HOUSE
AND
PHILOSOPHY

The Blackwell Philosophy and Pop Culture Series

Series Editor: William Irwin

South Park and Philosophy
Edited by Robert Arp

Metallica and Philosophy
Edited by William Irwin

Family Guy and Philosophy
Edited by J. Jeremy Wisnewski

The Daily Show and Philosophy
Edited by Jason Holt

Lost and Philosophy
Edited by Sharon Kaye

24 and Philosophy
*Edited by Jennifer Hart Weed,
Richard Davis, and Ronald Weed*

Battlestar Galactica and Philosophy
Edited by Jason T. Eberl

The Office and Philosophy
Edited by J. Jeremy Wisnewski

Batman and Philosophy
*Edited by Mark D. White and
Robert Arp*

House and Philosophy
Edited by Henry Jacoby

Watchmen and Philosophy
Edited by Mark D. White

X-Men and Philosophy
*Edited by Rebecca Housel and
J. Jeremy Wisnewski*

Terminator and Philosophy
*Edited by Richard Brown and
Kevin Decker*

Heroes and Philosophy
Edited by David Kyle Johnson

Twilight and Philosophy
*Edited by Rebecca Housel and
J. Jeremy Wisnewski*

Final Fantasy and Philosophy
*Edited by Jason P. Blahuta and
Michel S. Beaulieu*

Alice in Wonderland and
Philosophy
Edited by Richard Brian Davis

Iron Man and Philosophy
Edited by Mark D. White

True Blood and Philosophy
*Edited by George Dunn and
Rebecca Housel*

Mad Men and Philosophy
*Edited by James South and Rod
Carveth*

30 Rock and Philosophy
Edited by J. Jeremy Wisnewski

The Ultimate Harry Potter and
Philosophy
Edited by Gregory Bassham

HOUSE
AND
PHILOSOPHY
EVERYBODY
LIES

Edited by
Henry Jacoby

WILEY

John Wiley & Sons, Inc.

Published by John Wiley & Sons, Inc., Hoboken, New Jersey
Published simultaneously in Canada

For general information about our other products and services, please contact our Customer Care Department within the United States at (800) 762-2974, outside the United States at (317) 572-3993 or fax (317) 572-4002.

Wiley also publishes its books in a variety of electronic formats. Some content that appears in print may not be available in electronic books. For more information about Wiley products, visit our web site at www.wiley.com.

Library of Congress Cataloging-in-Publication Data:

House and philosophy : everybody lies / edited by Henry Jacoby.
  p.   cm. — (The Blackwell philosophy and pop culture series)
Includes index.
ISBN 978-0-470-31660-3 (pbk.)
  1. House, M. D.   I. Jacoby, Henry.
PN1992.77.H63H65   2008
791.45'72—dc22
                                                    2008016842

Printed in the United States of America

10 9 8 7

CONTENTS

ACKNOWLEDGMENTS

What? You Want Me
to Thank You?

First, I want to thank Bill Irwin for giving me the opportunity to work on this book. I couldn't have done it without his guidance, patient help, and consistent sage advice. Bill, you're truly one of the good guys, and it has been a pleasure to work with you.

Thanks to Jeff Dean, who first got things rolling. Since then, Connie Santisteban and all the nice people at Wiley have been great to work with. Thanks for all your help and support throughout this project.

I'm grateful to my fellow philosophers who contributed their wonderful essays. Your good work made my job easy.

My great friend and fellow guitar god Alan Berman actually read what I wrote and made creative suggestions. Not only that, he was always there when needed.

Without the talented people who work on *House*, there, of course, would be no book to write. Thanks for your brilliant hour of intelligent entertainment each week.

At home, my two cats, Bunkai and Willow, helped a lot, mostly by sleeping so I could work. They also took turns sitting with me when I needed inspiration. They are true Zen Masters.

Finally, there's my wife, Kathryn. Sweeter than Cameron, more patient than Wilson. And she helps with the typing. I can't do any of it without you.

INTRODUCTION

Read Less, More TV: A Cranky, Slightly Rude Introduction

Henry Jacoby

Dr. Gregory House, that brilliant pill-popping bastard, limps along the halls of Princeton-Plainsboro Teaching Hospital, knocking aside medical ethics with a wave of his cane. He tells us that everybody lies, that humanity is overrated, and that it's the nature of medicine that you're going to screw up. And one more thing: Read less, more TV! Yeah, House says that, too. But he wasn't talking about *this book*. You really should read this book, the one you're now holding in your hands. House would want you to.

But why should we listen to him? Isn't he a jerk? Well, yes, but unlike the guy standing next to you reading the book on intelligent design, House is cool. House plays a mean guitar and a killer piano, and chicks think he's sexy (it's the blue eyes). He even had a pet rat named Steve McQueen—how cool is that? And one more thing: he's brilliant. So who cares if he thinks that seizures are fun to watch but boring to diagnose? What's not to love?

I love House, and so do the contributors to this volume. Humanity may in fact be overrated, but not this bunch! I never once thought about firing them all and holding auditions for a new team. But more on them in a minute (they can wait, just like the clinic patients House ignores). Let's get back to the "What's not to love?" question.

Have I forgotten about the rudeness and the way House ridicules everyone else's ideas? (I tried that, by the way. I thought maybe I'd be branded an eccentric genius and be paid accordingly. It didn't work.) Have I forgotten that he's a drug addict? Have I forgotten that he once asked if it was still illegal to perform an autopsy on a living person? No, I haven't forgotten these things, but remember, he also saves lives. As Dr. Cuddy pointed out to that nasty Tritter fellow, he saves a lot more lives than he loses.

Like Socrates and Sherlock Holmes, House is intrigued by puzzles. His stubborn, relentless desire for the truth combined with his extraordinary reasoning skills means that the puzzles get solved, while the lives get saved. Hospital rules be damned!

Speaking of reasoning and truth, House has a lot to say about philosophy as well. And isn't it time that I got around to the philosophy part of *House and Philosophy* anyway? For House, Occam's Razor holds that the simplest explanation is that almost always somebody screwed up. How about reality? Philosophers argue a lot about that. House says that reality is almost always wrong. And the Socratic method! He loves that. He says it's the best way we have of teaching everything apart from juggling chainsaws.

The contributors to this volume (it's time to talk about them; they're not clinic patients, after all), just like House's team, are first-rate. They expertly expand on House's insights and examine his character. It's all in this book: Sartre and Nietzsche, Socrates and Aristotle, logic and luck, love and friendship, and even Zen. Some of it is pretty weird, really, but I like it. As House says, weird works for me. Now, bring me the thong of Lisa Cuddy!

PART ONE

"HUMANITY IS OVERRATED": HOUSE ON LIFE

SELFISH, BASE ANIMALS CRAWLING ACROSS THE EARTH: HOUSE AND THE MEANING OF LIFE

Henry Jacoby

We are selfish, base animals crawling across
the Earth. Because we got brains, we try real hard,
and we occasionally aspire to something that is less
than pure evil.

—"One Day, One Room"

So says Gregory House. It doesn't sound like he thinks life has any meaning, does it? Yet our Dr. House is leading what Socrates called "the examined life," and what Aristotle called "a life of reason," and such a life *is* a meaningful one. But how can this be? Could someone like House, who apparently thinks that life has no meaning, lead a meaningful life? And does House actually believe that our lives are meaningless?

"If You Talk to God, You're Religious; If God Talks to You, You're Psychotic"

Many people think that if there were no God, then life would have no meaning. So let's start there. Let's assume that our lives have meaning because we are fulfilling God's plan. In this case, meaning is constituted by a certain relationship with a spiritual being. If God does not exist, then our lives are meaningless. Or even if God does exist, but we're not related to Him in the right way, then again our lives are meaningless.

Perhaps God has a plan, and your life is meaningful to the extent that you help God realize that plan. For example, in the Kabbalah, the mystical writings of Judaism, we're supposed to be helping God repair the universe. This is a good example of what I mean; we're supposed to be helping God's plan succeed. A person who does this by doing good deeds and the like is thereby leading a meaningful life. Notice that someone could, in this view, lead a meaningful life, even if he believed that life had no meaning. Such a person might be doing God's work without realizing it. Could this be the sense in which House is leading a meaningful life?

Well, House doesn't believe in God; that's pretty clear. He consistently abuses those who do—for example, the Mormon doctor he calls "Big Love" in season four. In the season one episode "Damned If You Do," the patient, Sister Augustine, is a hypochondriac. As another Sister explains to House that "Sister Augustine believes in things that aren't real," House quips, "I thought that was a job requirement for you people." As another example, in "Family" House finds Foreman in the hospital chapel (Foreman is feeling remorse after having lost a patient), and he whispers, "You done talking to your imaginary friend? 'Cause I thought maybe you could do your job."

House's distaste for religion mostly stems from the lack of reason and logic behind religious belief. When Sister Augustine asks House, "Why is it so difficult for you to believe in God?"

he says, "What I have difficulty with is the whole concept of belief; faith isn't based on logic and experience." A further example occurs in season four ("The Right Stuff") when "Big Love" agrees to participate in an experiment that may save a patient's life. The experiment requires him to drink alcohol, which conflicts with his religious beliefs. He tells House that he was eventually persuaded by the reasoning behind House's request. "You made a good argument," he says. House is both impressed and surprised. "Rational arguments usually don't work on religious people," he says, "otherwise, there wouldn't be any religious people."

Reason, not faith, gets results in the real world. Again in "Damned If You Do," House berates Sister Augustine when she refuses medical treatment, preferring to leave her life in God's hands. "Are you trying to talk me out of my faith?" she asks. House responds: "You can have all the faith you want in spirits, and the afterlife, heaven and hell; but when it comes to this world, don't be an idiot. Because you can tell me that you put your faith in God to get you through the day, but when it comes time to cross the road I know you look both ways." Here House is hammering home the point that faith might provide comfort or make us feel good, but practical matters require reason and evidence.

Unlike many, House doesn't find religious belief— specifically, the idea of an afterlife—all that comforting. At one point he says, "I find it more comforting to believe that this [life] *isn't* simply a test" ("Three Stories").

Even putting aside House's views for the moment, there are serious problems with the idea that God dictates the meaning of our lives. Think of great scientists, who better our lives with their discoveries. Or humanitarians, who tirelessly work to improve the world. Or entertainers even—like Hugh Laurie!—who make our lives more enjoyable. Do we really want to say that if there's no God, then these accomplishments and goods don't count?

A further and fatal problem (first presented about a similar idea in Plato's dialogue *Euthyphro*, from which I now shamelessly borrow) is this: What makes God's plan meaningful in the first place? Is it meaningful simply *because* it's God's plan, or does God plan it *because it's meaningful?* If it's the former, then the plan is simply arbitrary. There's no reason behind it, and therefore it could just as easily have been the opposite! But this doesn't sit well. Surely not just any old thing could be meaningful.

Instead most would say God's plan is as it is *because God sees that such a course of events would be meaningful.* But if this is right, then something else (besides God's will) makes the plan meaningful. So the meaning in our lives has nothing to do with God. House is right about that (whether or not God exists).

Eternity, Anyone?

Perhaps just the fact that we have souls gives us intrinsic value and makes our lives meaningful. Or perhaps it has something to do with the idea that souls are supposed to be immortal and live on in an afterlife. If there is an afterlife, then *this life* is meaningful *because it's leading somewhere.*

But House no more believes in the soul than he does in God; and he's convinced there's no afterlife as well. No evidence, right? What about so-called near-death experiences? Do they provide evidence for the afterlife?

In the season four episode "97 Seconds," a patient tries to kill himself because he believes in the afterlife and wants to be there. He has already been clinically dead and brought back, and while "dead," he had "experiences" in a beautiful, peaceful afterlife. He says, "The paramedics said I was technically dead for 97 seconds. It was *the* best 97 seconds of my life." House, of course, won't stand for any of this. He tells the patient: "Okay, here's what happened. Your oxygen-deprived brain shutting down, flooded endorphins, serotonin, and gave you the visions."

In the same episode the afterlife theme comes up again as a dying cancer patient refuses the treatment that would prolong his painful life. He prefers death, and tells House and Wilson, "I've been trapped in this useless body long enough. It'd be nice to finally get out." House blasts back: "Get out and go where? You think you're gonna sprout wings and start flying around with the other angels? Don't be an idiot. There's no after, there is just this." Wilson and House then leave and have this wonderful exchange:

Wilson: You can't let a dying man take solace in his beliefs?

House: His beliefs are stupid.

Wilson: Why can't you just let him have his fairy tale if it gives him comfort to imagine beaches, and loved ones, and life outside a wheelchair?

House: There's 72 virgins, too?

Wilson: It's over. He's got days, maybe hours left. What pain does it cause him if he spends that time with a peaceful smile? What sick pleasure do you get in making damn sure he's filled with fear and dread?

House: He shouldn't be making a decision based on a lie. Misery is better than nothing.

Wilson: You don't know there's nothing; you haven't been there!

House: (rolls his eyes) Oh God, I'm tired of that argument. I don't have to go to Detroit to know that it smells!

But House, ever the scientist, wants proof. He's going to see for himself! He arranges to kill himself and is clinically dead for a short time before being brought back. At the end of the episode, he stands over the body of the patient, who has since died, and says, "I'm sorry to say . . . I told you so." What would House have said if there were an afterlife and God called him to account? Probably, "You should have given more evidence."[1]

Whether House's little experiment proved anything or not, what should we say about meaning and eternity? House, the philosopher, disagrees with the sentiment that life has to be leading somewhere to give it meaning. Consider this exchange between House and his patient Eve, who was raped, in the brilliant episode "One Day, One Room":

> House: If you believe in eternity, then life is irrelevant—the same as a bug is irrelevant in comparison to the universe.
>
> Eve: If you don't believe in eternity, then what you do here is irrelevant.
>
> House: Your acts here are all that matters.
>
> Eve: Then nothing matters. There's no ultimate consequences.

The patient expresses the idea that if this is all there is, then what's the point? But for House, if this is all there is, then what we do here is the only thing that matters. In fact, it makes it matter all that much more.

"If Her DNA Was Off by One Percentage Point, She'd Be a Dolphin"

Maybe our lives have no meaning. Maybe we *are* just crawling across the Earth, and nothing more. Someone could arrive at this conclusion two different ways. First, if meaning depends on God, the soul, or the afterlife, and none of these is real, then the conclusion follows. But also, if our lives are eternal, then, as House says, what we do in this limited time on Earth is diminished to the point of insignificance. From the point of view of an infinite universe, moreover, how can our little scurryings about amount to much of anything?

Philosophers who think that life is meaningless are called nihilists. To avoid nihilism, it seems we should stop worrying about God and the afterlife—and House, remember, rejects these anyway—and instead try to find meaning in our finite lives in the natural world. As House says, "Our actions here are all that matters."

How about how we *feel* about our actions? Does that matter? If a person feels that she's not accomplishing her goals, for example, or not having a positive impact on society, she might feel that her life has little or no meaning. But if she feels good about what she's doing, if it matters *to her*, might we not say that she's leading a meaningful life?

No, this is too easy. A person might be getting everything he wants, but if those wants are trivial, irrational, or evil, then it's hard to see this adding up to a meaningful life. For example, imagine someone like House who only watched soaps and played video games, but was not also a brilliant diagnostician busy saving lives. That would be a life without much meaning, even though our non-doctor version of House here might be perfectly content with his life.

Not only does "meaningful" not equal "getting what you want," but "meaningless" isn't the same as "not getting what you want." We might again imagine someone like House or even the real House himself: a terrific doctor helping a lot of people and saving lives, yet miserable, and not getting what he wants out of life at all. Yet, his life would still be meaningful and important because of its accomplishments, even though it didn't "feel" that way to him.

Now what if you care about things that are not trivial, irrational, or evil? Then, perhaps, your life could be meaningful to you—*subjectively*, as philosophers say—and at the same time be meaningful in the world, apart from your feelings, or *objectively*. So the question becomes this: What sort of life can we lead that produces meaning in both of these senses? And is our Dr. House leading such a life?

"You Could Think I'm Wrong, but That's No Reason to Stop Thinking"

Socrates (469–399 BCE), the first great hero of Western philosophy, was found guilty of corrupting the youth of Athens and not believing in the gods. For his crimes he was condemned to death. In actuality, Socrates was being punished for his habit of questioning others and exposing their ignorance in his search for truth. The jury would've been happy just to have him leave Athens, but Socrates declined that possibility, because he knew that his way of life would continue wherever he was.

Well, why not just change, then? In Plato's dialogue *Apology*, which describes the trial of Socrates, we hear Socrates utter the famous phrase "The unexamined life is not worth living." Socrates was telling us that he would rather die than give up his lifestyle. Why? What *is* an examined life anyway?

An examined life is one in which you seek the truth. You are curious. You want to understand. You do not just accept ideas because they are popular or traditional; you are not afraid to ask questions. This is the life of the philosopher.

The great British philosopher Bertrand Russell (1872–1970) described the value of this lifestyle and the value of philosophy in general when he wrote:

> Philosophy is to be studied, not for the sake of any definite answers to its questions, since no definite answers can, as a rule, be known to be true, but rather for the sake of the questions themselves; because these questions enlarge our conception of what is possible, enrich our intellectual imagination and diminish the dogmatic assurance which closes the mind against speculation.[2]

Surely House agrees with this. In the episode "Resignation" House finally figures out what's killing a young girl, and he tries to tell her. Since this information will not change the fact that she's going to die, she has no interest in hearing what he has to say. "I don't want to hear it," she says. House is incredulous: "This is what's killing you; you're not interested in what's killing you?" As her parents make him leave the room, he says, "What's the point in living without curiosity?" Sounds a lot like Socrates.

Now maybe a life of curiosity—the philosopher's life (or the scientist who's interested in knowledge for its own sake)—is a valuable life, and maybe it's better than "an unexamined life." But that hardly means that an unexamined life isn't worth living at all. Why does Socrates think that? And why does House imply that such a life is pointless?

The examined life is the life of the philosopher, a life of reason. And reason is what is distinctive about humans. When Aristotle (384–322 BCE) said that "man is a rational animal," he didn't mean that we are always rational and never emotional or instinctive. He meant that humans alone have the *capacity* for reason. I think Socrates's point, then, is that a person who doesn't use reason, who doesn't lead an examined life, isn't realizing his potential as a human being. A life without reason and curiosity, a life where one doesn't seek the truth, is therefore a life no greater than the life of a lower animal.

House probably wouldn't put it quite like that. Remember, he thinks that "humanity is overrated." Still, a life where his puzzle-solving skills are put to no good use would be a life he would find incredibly dull and pointless.

House and the Life of Reason

It may be true that the unexamined life is a life without meaning and, therefore, not worth living, but that doesn't mean that *the examined life is meaningful* (and worth living). After all, the nihilists could be right. Maybe no life is ever really meaningful. Maybe no life is ever really worth living. How can we decide?

To answer this, we must return to the question of what makes a life meaningful. We must explain the properties that a meaningful life has, and then show that the Socratic examined life has those properties. From what we've seen so far, and especially where House is concerned, these properties have nothing to do with God, the soul, or the afterlife. They may, however, have something to do with how one feels about one's life, as long as those feelings match up with what we ought to care about, what we ought to feel is important.

House's life is meaningful because he, for the most part, brings about desirable consequences. He saves lives. But the problem is, he doesn't seem to care that much about the lives he saves. For him, it's more about solving the puzzle. Why? Because that satisfies him? And it takes away his pain?

It's more than that. By solving puzzles, and thereby saving lives, House is exemplifying the life of reason. And this is what Aristotle deemed to be our proper function.

Aristotle was trying to answer the question "What is the good life?" For him, *good* is defined by a thing's proper function. For example, a good cane would be one that was easy to grip, helped you keep your balance, and kept you from further injury and pain while walking; a good doctor would be a doctor who was able to properly and efficiently diagnose and treat diseases (among other things). A good life then would be the kind of life that a good person would lead. So what is a good person? What is humanity's proper function?

We've already seen the answer: it comes from leading the life of reason. For Aristotle, this amounts to the rational part of us controlling the irrational part. The irrational part of us contains our desires; it tells us what we want and what we don't want. I like Thai food; I hate lima beans. This is how it works. But it doesn't tell us how much or how often we should want what we want. The irrational part, says Aristotle, contains no principle of measurement.

Reason, however, can measure, can discern proper amounts. These "proper amounts" are the virtues. For example, consider courage. Someone who is easily angered and always ready to fight does not possess courage. But neither does the coward. Courage is, as Plato had already noted, "knowing when to fight and when not to." Wilson, for example, often displays courage in his dealings with House, his friend. He knows when to stand up to him, but he also knows when to say nothing and avoid anger.

Just using reason in any old way is, of course, not the same as leading a rational life. Solving sudoku puzzles certainly requires logic and reasoning skills, but someone who did nothing else with his life would not thereby be living rationally. House's prodigious puzzle-solving skills, on the other hand, *are* meaningful and important, because of the results that they help to produce. Reason must be properly tied to action; House understands this. Again from "One Day, One Room" when Eve, the rape victim, says, "Time changes everything," House replies, "It's what people say; it's not true. Doing things changes things; not doing things leaves things exactly as they were."

Living the life of reason is, finally, of ultimate importance, according to Aristotle, because it leads to happiness or well-being—what the Greeks termed *eudaimonia*. So even if House usually seems to care more about solving the puzzles than the results that ensue, solving the puzzles must contribute to some sense of internal well-being for him, if I am right that he's living the examined life, the life of reason.

Some people would no doubt disagree with this conclusion. House, after all, they might say, seems to be miserable. Paraphrasing the sexy nutritionist from season three's "Resignation," I say to them: How miserable can he be saving lives, sleeping around, and doing drugs? Pass Aristotle the Vicodin.

NOTES

1. This is what Bertrand Russell said in a famous anecdote. I imagine House might add: "And as long as we're here, how come bad things happen to puppies? Cameron wants to know."

2. Bertrand Russell, *The Problems of Philosophy* (Oxford: Oxford Univ. Press, 1976), 161.

HOUSE AND SARTRE: "HELL IS OTHER PEOPLE"

Jennifer L. McMahon

When it first aired in the fall of 2004, the Fox series *House* seemed an unlikely hit. Focusing its attention on the brilliant but deeply unlikable Dr. Gregory House, it left little room for the audience to see the show's protagonist as anything but a jerk. But several years and several Golden Globes later, *House* is a huge success. What is the source of *House*'s appeal? As a medical drama, it draws upon our deep-seated cultural interest in medicine. Centered on the investigation of mysterious maladies with a protagonist modeled on the legendary Sherlock Homes, it also satisfies our long-standing fascination with detective stories. But *House* is more than another *ER*, more than another *CSI*. Its singularity lies primarily in its surprising protagonist, a man who simultaneously inspires interest and loathing. *House* is like a car wreck—you can't help but look. While, thankfully, most of us don't come upon car wrecks every day, *House* illustrates something we do encounter daily: irritating people.

Sartre's Theory of Others: A Case History

House has an important predecessor in its focus on the negativity of social relations. The existential philosopher Jean-Paul Sartre (1905–1980) is well known for his cynical account of interpersonal relationships, as manifested in both his philosophy and his literary works. Known for his analysis of the oppressive nature of "the look"[1] and for the declaration "Hell is other people,"[2] Sartre highlights the anxiety that our relationships with others elicit and the way those relationships can inhibit personal autonomy. While Sartre regards interpersonal relations as tremendous sources of conflict and concern, he is also emphatic that these relationships are essential to our being. Sartre's theory of others is conveyed in his principal philosophic work *Being and Nothingness* and in his play *No Exit*. Sartre's account of social relationships contrasts with that of his contemporary and fellow existentialist Martin Heidegger (1889–1976). While both Sartre and Heidegger regard humans as fundamentally social beings, Heidegger emphasizes the sense of connection people experience. In contrast, Sartre emphasizes how others frequently irritate and impede us, and he asserts that the relations that exist between individuals are fundamentally ones of "conflict."[3] He attributes the ambivalence we experience toward others to three main causes.

The first reason that others arouse negative feelings in us is that they represent potential obstacles to our freedom. According to Sartre, without interference from others, individuals are typically absorbed in existence, particularly in the task of obtaining the things that they need and desire from the environment. Rather than thinking about their experience, they are immersed in it. They act without reflecting. As Sartre explains, the appearance of another person pulls the individual out of this original state of absorption. The appearance of another comes not only as a surprise, but also as a threat. Other people are threatening because life is such that individuals must procure resources for survival and satisfaction. Because the resources we strive to obtain are not infinite in quantity, others are fundamentally competitors, not colleagues. Moreover, while objects can resist acquisition by the individual, they do not normally inhibit an individual's autonomy; however, other people frequently do. Unlike inert objects, people can actively challenge the individual by denying her access to resources, inhibiting her activity, or most obviously, by attacking her person.

The threat that others present to the individual is evident in *House* in a variety of ways. House himself does virtually everything he can to antagonize his colleagues and patients. This is particularly evident in the relationships that he has with the young physicians he oversees. Though employed at a teaching hospital and charged with the task of supervising three promising specialists, House is anything but a nurturing presence in the lives of Drs. Cameron, Foreman, and Chase and the cadre of candidates who strive to replace the original team in season four. Instead, he mocks, berates, and intentionally confounds them. Their education under the tutelage of the famous diagnostician takes the form of an ongoing psychological assault as House actively tries to sabotage their confidence and self-esteem. While House's treatment of his subordinates is reprehensible, he exemplifies the threat that others pose in another, even more blatant way. Important to our understanding of his character and essential to our ability to sympathize with him is the fact that we ultimately attribute most of House's malignancy toward others to his own pain.

Another reason that Sartre contends that others inspire negative feelings has to do with the way they objectify us. While every individual is a composite of mind and body, Sartre believes that individuals identify more closely with their minds than with their bodies. While individuals tend to think of themselves more as agents than as objects, others serve as painful reminders that we are physical beings, bodies with properties.

Through their looks and their verbal appraisals, people remind us—often painfully—that we are physical beings when they remark on our weight, comment on our height, or look disapprovingly at our clothes. We objectify people primarily because we do not (and cannot) experience their minds but can only perceive and interact with them primarily as objects. And being an object is troubling because knowing that one is a concrete some*thing* clearly limits one's freedom to be or do anything, and it is characteristic of human consciousness to resist any sort of confinement that it hasn't chosen.

Once again *House* illustrates Sartre's theory. Our tendency to regard individuals as objects is most apparent in House's treatment of patients, particularly the patients at the clinic. Because they do not suffer from the enigmatic sorts of illnesses that he treats in his lab, such patients hold no allure for House. Consequently, he treats them like vermin. Forced by Dr. Cuddy to keep clinic hours, House does nothing to disguise his disdain for the common man. Though Cuddy hopes that "if House deals with enough people he'll find some humanity," patients simply serve as the means by which House can pursue his occupation. In the case of clinic patients, they are obstacles. To clear a return path to the haven of the diagnostics lab, House will lie to, sedate, and even prematurely discharge these run-of-the-mill patients. For example, in "One Day, One Room," he goes so far as to offer money to one patient to forgo treatment, and he prescribes another a drug that causes paralysis in order to control his screaming. When asked by Cuddy why he would administer a drug that only stops the latter patient's behavior but does not alleviate his pain, House responds nonchalantly, "Someone had to stop the screaming." For House, the patient was like an irritating car alarm that needed to be silenced.

Sartre's last reason that others compel feelings of antagonism is that they rob the individual of her sense of primacy and control. As we all know, other people do not necessarily do what we want. They have their own agendas. They also do not necessarily share our beliefs or our sense of what is important. Indeed, they may see the world in a radically different way than we do, and they normally resist our efforts to turn them to our advantage. We don't like this! Sartre uses several graphic images to illustrate the impact that the appearance of other consciousnesses has on the psyche of the individual. Using a medical metaphor, he asserts that the presence of others creates a "hemorrhage"[4] in the individual's world, a fissure that causes the world that the individual knows to "disintegrate."[5] Similarly, he describes the other as the "drainhole"[6] through which the individual's sense of the world and sense of security are lost.

In *House*, patients in the diagnostics lab challenge the expertise of their physicians while Dr. Gregory House challenges both his patients' and his colleagues' beliefs about the practice of medicine. A maverick in both attitude and action, House ruffles everyone's feathers. He constantly bucks the authority of his superiors and turns his subordinates' expectations on their heads. Much to the chagrin of his associates, he frequently breaches the bounds of professional and personal ethics. Take House's decision to use electroshock therapy to wipe out the memory of a young firefighter who was stricken with life-threatening heart attacks, catalyzed by the presence of his unrequited love ("Words and Deeds"). Though the treatment stops the instances of cardiac arrest, it comes at great cost. House literally erases substantial portions of this man's life and identity, portions that we later realize may not have needed removal.

Others: A Painful Need

While others create profound feelings of anxiety and concern, Sartre is nonetheless clear that we need others. Individuals need both the care of, and interaction with, others in order to develop the cognitive abilities, emotional repertoire, and moral attributes we see as essentially human. While Sartre is strangely silent on the most obvious way in which humans are dependent upon others, namely the physiological dependence of infants and children on caregivers, he is clear that without interaction with others, we would not have language, self-awareness, or an objective identity.

In *House*, the dependence that individuals have on one another is made evident through the medium of medicine. Patients who go to Princeton-Plainsboro need medical care, care they cannot provide themselves. The patients placed with House's diagnostics team are an even more obvious example of dependence. Affected with illnesses that other physicians have been unable to diagnose or treat, they depend on House for their survival. Of course, this is why they (and House's colleagues) are willing to put up with House. Despite his drug addiction, his abrasive personality, and his defiance of authority, he is simply too good a physician to lose. Too many lives depend on him.

When it comes to the dependence we have on others, the emergence of self-awareness and personal identity are of special interest to Sartre. According to Sartre, interaction with others is necessary to the emergence of reflective consciousness. Prior to engagement with others, individuals are conscious, but they are not self-conscious. Effectively illustrating his point with the example of someone absorbed in the act of spying through a keyhole until someone spots him from behind and turns him into an object,[7] Sartre argues that it is only through encounters with others that we are brought to fully realized self-consciousness.

House illustrates the role others play in the development of self-consciousness as well. The members of House's team hold the key to their patients' awareness of themselves, and in diagnosing ailments, these physicians simultaneously heighten their patients' self-consciousness. Interestingly, through their interaction, Cuddy, Wilson, Cameron, Foreman, Chase, and even House are more reflective and self-aware because of one another's presence.

While extraordinarily important in itself, self-consciousness is also essential to the development of an objective identity. To have a self means to have in one's mind an objective sense of oneself, a sense of one's characteristics, aptitudes, and likes and dislikes. Sartre does not believe that individuals can develop selves on their own, but rather argues that others play an integral role in the consolidation of personal identity. As Sartre states, "The Other holds . . . the secret of what I am."[8] Developmentally speaking, individuals obtain their sense of self initially through the assimilation of objective characterizations supplied by others. For example, children who are told (and treated like) they are worthless come to believe they are. Though others are most influential in early childhood and adolescence, Sartre is clear that the role that others play in identity formation does not end when individuals reach adulthood. Rather, our identities are shaped by the social relations we have throughout our lives. Our personalities are forged reciprocally through social interaction, first through assimilation, and later through more critical appropriation and projection of the objective characterizations we supply one another. Drs. Cameron, Foreman, and Chase are likewise shaped by their interactions with House and with one another. Though not always (or even typically) pleasant, their interactions prompt each of them to develop in important ways as physicians and as people.

The final way Sartre says we depend on others is less flattering, if not less pervasive. As Sartre indicates, others arouse as much antagonism in us as empathy. For this reason, we often would prefer to resist than engage with them. Yet, in dealing with life's difficulties, Sartre is clear that others can serve as convenient sources of consolation. As Sartre makes clear in *Being and Nothingness*, others are by no means the only things that individuals find profoundly disturbing. Instead, we are as horrified at our freedom as we are excited about it, as anxious about the absence of meaning as we are thrilled with the prospect of making it, and as terrified of life as we are of death. Because of all of the anxieties that affect us, Sartre describes human life as a "troubled longing"[9] and contends that the standard response that most people take to their existential anxiety is "flight."[10]

Sartre uses the term "bad faith" to refer to the varied efforts that individuals take to escape disturbing aspects of the human condition. Interestingly, relationships with others figure both as a means to bad faith projects as well as motivations for them. Because of the deep-seated anxiety that individuals experience with respect to social relations, Sartre asserts that honest and mutually productive—what he would call "authentic"—interpersonal relationships are a rarity (if not an impossibility). Instead, most people never get beyond seeing others as objects, or using others to avoid responsibility by letting those others reduce them to "the mode of being a thing."[11] This tendency to try and be subject or object but not both leads Sartre to suggest that far from being an anomaly, most relationships are sadomasochistic in character.[12]

House illustrates both the human propensity toward bad faith as well as the sadist's method of escaping authentic relationships with others. Ultimately, bad faith involves denial, specifically denial of some aspect of one's condition. As Sartre states, bad faith is "a lie to oneself"[13] in which the goal is escape. In the case of House, rather than take responsibility for his addiction and his callous treatment of others, he instead conveniently assumes the role of the victim and uses his infirmity to justify both his drug abuse and his general insensitivity.

With respect to his treatment of others, and perhaps because of the trauma and loss he has experienced, House resists connecting with others. Instead, he alienates anyone who tries to get close to him with his antisocial behavior and speech. Like the sadist Sartre describes as being deeply fearful of the vulnerability that authentic relationships to others entail, House refuses genuine sociality by "mak[ing] an object out of [the other]."[14] Where authentic relationships require that one recognize and respect the freedom of others and the depth of one's connection to them, House, like the sadist, creates the illusion of absolute independence by seeing others "[as] those forms which pass by in the street . . . [and by acting] as if [he] were alone."[15] House also illustrates the tendency of the sadist not merely to derive security from objectifying others, but to derive even greater satisfaction by making himself the individual upon whom other individuals depend.[16] Effectively making himself into a god (which Sartre contends is virtually everyone's deep-seated wish), both House and the sadist savor the dependence that others have on them while remaining comfortably aloof from the uncomfortable demands of reciprocity. Of course, it's no mystery why House would prefer to objectify others rather than contemplate his own objective nature. Who would want to admit the fact that he is a depressed, drug-addicted, socially maladjusted genius with chronic pain and a permanent physical disability?

One Room, One Hell

Sartre illustrates the antagonistic and essential nature of others in his dark comedy No Exit. The setting and message of this play are strikingly similar to the episode "One Day, One Room." Set in hell rather than in a hospital, Sartre's play conveys both the dependence individuals have on others as well as the acute anxiety and antagonism they can elicit from one another. It also portrays in amusing terms the sadomasochistic tendencies to which Sartre contends we are all subject. The play opens with Garcin's arrival in hell. Garcin, who finds himself in hell after being executed for desertion, is surprised to find hell a stuffy and poorly decorated room rather than an endless chasm of torture. Of course, Garcin's torture comes. It arrives in the form of two women, Inez and Estelle. The remainder of the play consists in Sartre's ingenious portrayal of this ménage à trois, a ménage where no one gets laid and everyone suffers.

Sartre's cynicism regarding relationships is obvious in the play. It is made most obvious through his choice of setting: hell. Though it doesn't fit the conventional depiction, Sartre's hell is torturous. The hell in which Garcin, Inez, and Estelle are placed is a room from which there is no escape, principally no escape from each other. As the play makes clear, existence is hell, and it is made hellish by the fact that it is shared with others. Small details like the absence of windows, the denial of sleep, and the absence of eyelids further reinforce the inescapability and negativity of social relationships. The characters in Sartre's play literally have no reprieve from one another, not the consolation of a glance out of doors, the solipsistic bliss of slumber, not even the brief respite granted when "the shutter[s]"[17] of one's eyes close. No, Sartre's characters are "inseparables"[18] who sense each other, every second, in "every pore."[19]

The episode "One Day, One Room" contains insights about interpersonal relations analogous to those found in *No Exit*. Indeed, insofar as Eve, the primary patient, was a philosophy and comparative religion major, one wonders whether Sartre's text was the inspiration for some of the dialogue. In this episode, House is once again forced by Cuddy to take cases in the clinic. After seeing multiple patients who suspect they have STDs and after declaring that he is "tired of wiping crotches," House reluctantly enters into a series of conversations with one of those patients, Eve, a young college graduate who was raped.

The first parallel with *No Exit* is that, with one exception, all of the interactions between Eve and House take place within the confines of an exam room, a place that neither of them wanted, or chose, to be in. Like Garcin, Inez, and Estelle, Eve and House find themselves in a social situation they cannot escape. Like Sartre's trio, Eve and House also find each other unpleasant. With his standard callousness, House provides little comfort to Eve. With no exotic malady to treat, only a trauma for which House contends there is no cure, Eve holds no interest for House. Indeed, to the extent she is a mirror image of his own trauma, a trauma from which he has tried to dissociate, Eve is a patient House wants to escape. Eve offers House no such avenue. In a surprising move, rather than flee House herself, Eve requests that he be her physician. Here, Eve's choice is analogous to Sartre's characters' decision to stay in hell when given the opportunity to leave. Though House says he will prove "useless" at helping her, he elects to continue as well.

Like *No Exit*, the episode illustrates both people's dependence upon others and their disdain for them. For example, when Eve repeatedly asks House to tell her about his experience, House is made visibly uncomfortable. When he lies to placate her and she calls him on it, House becomes so frustrated that he sedates Eve in order to thwart her efforts to get him to open up. Here, unlike Sartre's characters, who are denied the chance to escape others through the medium of sleep, House has a whole pharmacy at his disposal.

While Eve is sedated, House inadvertently reveals his need for others as he solicits each of his colleagues for advice. In a surprising reversal of roles, House goes first to Wilson, then to Cameron, Foreman, and Chase, to ask each one to tell him what to say to Eve. Amusingly, they all tell him different things. Laughably, Chase even advises that House "keep her asleep." Happily, House does let Eve wake up, and their subsequent conversation proves productive for both of them.

As her name suggests, Eve is the first woman in the series who really gets House to let down his guard. Though he puts up resistance, House eventually opens up to Eve and tells her his story. What prompts House to do so, in part, is an exchange that the two have about people. Urging Eve not to rely on him, House asks her, "You going to base your whole life on who you got stuck in a room with?" Echoing Inez's line, "You are your life, nothing else,"[20] Eve responds, "It's what life is. It's a series of rooms. And who we get stuck with in those rooms adds up to what our lives are." The second-to-last scene of the episode then places House and Eve not in a room, but outside, sitting together in the park, finally connecting with each other. The volume drops. We do not hear what they are saying. The implication is that it's not what they say to each other that is important, but the fact that they are interacting with each other, that there is reciprocity. The tension that has been evident between them is absent. Like the laughter that echoes as the curtains close in *No Exit*, the final impression is positive.

Ultimately, *House* illustrates the antagonistic nature of social relations primarily through the means of its misanthropic protagonist, Dr. Gregory House. It illustrates the dependency we have on others through the medium of medicine. Characteristic of the show is that House's patients depend upon him quite literally for their being. Thus, like Sartre's *Being and Nothingness* and his play *No Exit*, *House* reinforces the message that humans need others not only in obvious physical ways, but also in more subtle, but equally important, psychological ones. While others engender anxiety, they also define who we are. From infancy to death, our relationships with others shape our personalities and help determine the real potentialities that we possess as individuals. Though others can enrage, exploit, even endanger us, they are also essential to our being. They help us see ourselves as we are, an endeavor that, while sometimes excruciating, actually furthers our freedom by making us more fully informed. Using a medical metaphor himself, Sartre asserts that the world is "infected" with others. Similarly, *House* depicts the presence of others as both an ontological malady and a necessity.

NOTES

1. Jean-Paul Sartre, *Being and Nothingness*, trans. Hazel E. Barnes (New York: Washington Square Press, 1956), 340.

2. Jean-Paul Sartre, *No Exit*, in *No Exit and Three Other Plays*, trans. Stuart Gilbert (New York: Vintage International Press, 1989), 45.

3. Ibid., 475.

4. Ibid., 345.

5. Ibid., 342.

6. Ibid., 343.

7. Ibid., 347.

8. Ibid., 475.

9. Ibid., 503.

10. Ibid., 78.

11. Ibid., 99.

12. Ibid., 490–495. Here, Sartre uses the term *sadomasochism* to refer to relationships in which one party takes a subordinate role, and effectively assumes the role of an object insofar as he or she lets the other party in the relationship determine his or her role or function. Though sexual relationships qualify, Sartre does not use the term sadomasochism to refer exclusively—or even primarily—to sexual relationships.

13. Ibid., 89.

14. Ibid., 473.

15. Ibid., 495.

16. Ibid., 482.

17. Ibid., 5.

18. Ibid., 42.

19. Ibid., 22.

20. Ibid., 43.

IS THERE A SUPERMAN
IN THE HOUSE?:
A NIETZSCHEAN POINT
OF VIEW

David Goldblatt

I teach you the Übermensch. Man is something
that should be overcome. What have you done to
overcome him?

—Nietzsche's Zarathustra

To Nietzsche these Übermenschen appear as symbols
of the repudiation of any conformity to a single norm:
antithesis to mediocrity and stagnation.

—Walter Kaufmann

Had their paths ever crossed, Friedrich Nietzsche (1844–1900)
might well have become a patient of Dr. Gregory House.
Nietzsche suffered from a mixture of undiagnosed diseases

and bouts of depression throughout his life—just the kind of unusual case House handles week after week at the fictional Princeton-Plainsboro Teaching Hospital. Nietzsche's symptoms and ailments included severe migraines exacerbated by extreme eyestrain, painful nausea, colic, diphtheria, and dysentery. Haunting him virtually his entire life, these maladies intensified during his debilitated years (1874–1876) and culminated in "a literal collapse," forcing him to leave his teaching position. Nietzsche writes at this time: "I could no longer doubt that I am suffering from a serious brain illness, and that my eyes and stomach only suffered as a result of this central process."[1] Ten years before his death in 1900, Nietzsche lapsed into an undefined madness from which he did not recover.

Nietzsche may be most famous for his controversial concept of the *Übermensch*, translated as "superman" or "overman," a figure of great achievement but, more important, of noble or superior character, self-assured with a will to "overcome" a conforming and constricting gravity of custom and morality. Does this sound like our Dr. House? Could he be an example of what Nietzsche had in mind?

Men and Supermen

On the one hand, Nietzsche often writes as if there are no current supermen—the superman belongs to the future: "Never yet has there been an *Übermensch*," says Nietzsche's fictional character Zarathustra. So the overman remains an ideal type— what the human species only potentially can become: "Man is a rope tied between beast and *Übermensch*."[2] Nietzsche often suggests that the course of an entire culture, even a mediocre society, is justified if it produces just a *few* superior beings.

On the assumption that no one presently meets the criteria for the overman, then, of course, House could not. However, what Nietzsche sometimes imagines for some future superior class, he suggests has already happened somewhat by accident in individuals from many different spheres of our culture—religious, military, and artistic. Among them we can find the names Napoleon, Goethe, Jesus, Caesar, and Shakespeare. If we are to consider Dr. House in this context, we need to think of his hospital as a microcosm of the world at large and House, an individual of obvious achievement and influence, relative to that environment.

Nietzsche is more provocateur than prophet. Of course, so is House. Nietzsche's words are often charges against his readers and challenges to them to act in ways that defy the norm. Man is something that needs to be overcome, and Zarathustra asks of everyone and no one, "What have you done to overcome him?" What have you done to move beyond the ordinary, to become more like this superior being?

House's Character

House as teacher can be seen in two ways. First, there is the House who works his diagnostic magic, solving special cases for the sake of solving alone, much like one might attempt a crossword puzzle. We can imagine this House indifferent to the education of his staff and not particularly interested in the welfare of the patients.

Second, there is the House who teaches *character*. House isn't offering additional medical knowledge alone. Rather, from House, his young staff can learn the virtues of the overman, which are not to be found in *Gray's Anatomy*. House wants his staff to think independently, to "overcome" their previous education. To do this they will need a special kind of courage—the courage to stand up in the profession and voice objections over the desires of patients and in spite of restrictions imposed by their own superiors. House teaches the need for the energy and tenacity to look beyond the solutions found in the medical books, to resist the defeatism that often leads to wrong turns, and the willingness to take risks and to exercise imagination.

By example, House teaches blunt patient interview and insightful observation. House is often able to see that a patient is lying—out of fear or embarrassment. Or he can notice personality quirks that offer Holmesian clues to complex diseases. But unless House overturns standard analyses, he will fail the patient. He succeeds as teacher only if his pupils can see beyond the strictly medical, in a narrow sense of that word, and expand the traditional role of doctor. House exemplifies a doctor with the discipline and self-will to control and overcome the professional status quo. Eschewing professional rewards and inertia-laden contentment, House does not hesitate to act in underhanded ways to encourage the progress of his staff and to solve the often bizarre problems laid out for them.

The Double Standard

There is a double standard operating in each episode of *House*, as House is tolerated as an exception to hospital rules and regulations. This fits nicely with Nietzsche's conception of the overman: "He [Nietzsche] wanted to make room for an aristocratic morality designed for exceptions. And he sought to undermine the idea that there is *one* type of morality for all individuals, one dictatorial morality that prescribes how all humans ought to live."[3]

Believing House is somehow special, his colleagues enable and defend him despite his many violations of custom, tradition, and the law. We have seen House forge prescriptions, lie to almost everyone, and violate drug laws. But curiously, House doesn't justify his own behavior by appealing to his achievements and thus his value to others. It isn't a matter of self-entitlement— House is simply indifferent to confining rules, and if circumstances dictate, he acts as if the regulations did not exist.

House's Style

There is a definite aesthetic dimension to Nietzsche's work, and the artist is perhaps the best example of the overman. For the artist, creation is overcoming. However, the artist can become the artwork as the overman makes his own life a work of art.

Nietzsche emphasizes "giving style to one's character" as the substance of an outstanding life. The obvious prominence of style in the character of Dr. House leaves others at his hospital, which, for all their diversity, dress and speak in the same tentative modes, pale or sterile by comparison. Their range of emotional expressions and attempts at humor are nearly nonexistent when considered alongside House's adolescent antics and cutting words.

The stylistic pluralism of Nietzsche's writings is reflected in his contention that one can mold one's own life in accord with a number of different, but distinct, styles. Style is a complex and elusive matter, changing with change in context. That Gregory House doesn't dress, speak, or have the manners of a good hospital doctor is the most obvious mark of *House*. As a dramatic device, the strong style of House creates a constant tension between himself and the other characters while soliciting ambiguous admiration from the viewers. The aura of House's style serves as a visual and auditory symbol of this value—that he is defended and tolerated despite his appearance. We envy House for the unpretentious way he speaks his mind and for his guilt-free attitude in pushing across his own beliefs and desires. Nietzsche's overman is superior in the sense that he does not reference the world to determine who he is. Like House, the overman constructs his own identity.

On one interpretation the overman is valued in and for himself, not for what he may bring to the culture. Indeed, it is the culture that may form the soil for whatever the overman may become. On this note Walter Kaufmann says, "For Nietzsche, the Overman . . . is valuable in himself . . . and society is censured insofar as it insists on conformity and impedes his development."[4] If this is not quite the circumstance of Dr. House, it certainly would seem to reflect the attitude of the viewer toward House and perhaps even many of his colleagues, who are attracted to House for who he is—his blunt and witty talk, his rebellious and humorous attitude toward the all-too-serious hospital scene.

In addition, there may be an equally significant purpose to House's unique lifestyle. We, the viewers, may be asked to remember just what is important about doctoring and what is not—what is essential to the medical profession and what is mere accessory.

Denial

Not to be confused with the "aesthetic," Nietzsche's comments on the "ascetic"—the person who practices self-denial—are particularly surprising. One might think that the Nietzschean affirmation of bodily things would set him against the ascetic way of life. But Nietzsche offers the ascetic some small praise among his condemnations, something that seems to have come from Nietzsche's Asian influences. The self-imposed material restraints of the ascetic are really an attempt to preserve life, to fight for existence in a difficult and suffering world. So for Nietzsche, a world in which the human is a sickly animal, "the ascetic ideal is an artifice for the preservation of life. . . . You will see my point: this ascetic priest, this apparent enemy of life . . . is among the greatest *conserving* and yes-creating forces of life."[5] House, while not quite an ascetic, is almost never depicted as having or wanting the usual emblems of material success afforded to him by his profession. His motorcycle and jeans attest to his modest lifestyle. We don't see in House a conscious denial of consumer goods, only a lack of interest in them. And we see House, like the ascetic, as nonpolitical, immune to the politics of the hospital and the medical profession. What we see of his surroundings is modest and simple, without acquisitive habits.

Pain

In writing about pain, Georg Simmel (1858–1918) says, "This is one of the fundamental themes of the history of the human soul—the essential elevation of our being is effected through pain. . . . Nietzsche transfers this connection beyond the individual to mankind: only discipline attended by great pain has brought forth 'all elevation of humanity.'"[6] In a poetic sentence Nietzsche's Zarathustra says, "One must still have chaos within oneself to give birth to a dancing star." House's "chaos" seems to find its roots in his very real pain, which, according to at least one placebo-contrived episode, may be psychosomatic. The pain, whatever its cause, may be the detour directing House on the higher road to accomplishment via focus and intensity.

Nietzsche's earliest works, *The Birth of Tragedy out of the Spirit of Music* and *Philosophy in the Tragic Age of the Greeks*, radically reinterpret standard contemporary views regarding Greek philosophy and art. As M. S. Silk and J. P. Stern say, "The suffering hero of Greek tragedy, Oedipus or Prometheus, is the original model for Nietzsche's superman."[7] These mythological characters messed with gods, and because of their acts, they pay heavily and with physical pain. With House we encounter some obvious similarities with these Nietzschean models. House's achievements are remarkable if not mythological, and while they are for the good of others, House disregards standards of common courtesy and rules that have historically regulated the institution of medicine. House's pain, like that of Oedipus and Prometheus, engages our empathy and may be connected with his ability to solve problems unsolvable by most others, his "elevation." It would be easy to say that House's acerbic personality, quite unlike the overman, is an outgrowth of his pain and his abuse of others is a mode of relief. But what would a protagonist be without a flaw to move him just a little bit toward the role of underdog when his behavior seems to flow in the opposite direction?

Inheriting the Earth

The philosopher Martin Heidegger (1889–1976), who wrote extensively on Nietzsche, sees the overman's role as an answer to an overwhelming question: "Is man, as man in his nature till now, prepared to assume dominion over the whole earth?" Heidegger credits Nietzsche as "the first thinker who, in view of a world history emerging for the first time, asks the decisive question and thinks through its metaphysical implications."[8] If man is not prepared, he says, man must be brought beyond himself, and this Beyondman is some future type of being who can be delivered from revenge and has the will to free itself from the "it was," the past that can no longer be willed. It is a freedom from the past—its memory of guilt, shame, and bitterness brought on by European morality. House seems to have the capacity to disregard any guilt that would have been due to the offensive behavior he may have inflicted upon patients or colleagues. Instead he acts with flair, confidence, and careless indifference. So, then, the "over" in overman contains a negation for Heidegger—a negative affirmation steering our species away from what we are, creatures of revenge, to a new kind of future being. How does House fit with this account? Pretty well. House shows little if any sign of self-pity or resentment despite the bullet wounds he sustained and the bad luck causing his leg pain.

The Fiction

Is House's contempt for bureaucracy and his rejection of medical recipes in favor of instinct and intuition for uncannily getting things right a "bridge" between man and superman?

Can House really be a foreshadowing of a futuristic alternative to Western medicine and a willingness to escape the narrow historicity of the white-coated doctor's image? Clearly House's feats have no equivalent in the actual world of the hospital. House is a fiction within a fiction. The frequency of challenging, even bizarre, cases, his specialty and his *raison d'être* at the hospital where he works, and the ingenuity of his solutions are beyond the plausible. His demeanor and dress tend both to exaggerate his alien presence and to present him as a gritty anchor to an extra-medical world. And while his arrogance and abusive behavior may not be what Nietzsche had in mind by an *Übermensch*, his achievement and style, his strength of will, his absence of resentment, and his timely disregard for the conforming behaviors and moralities of others are well in line with Nietzsche's ideal.

NOTES

1. Quoted in Karl Pletsch, *Young Nietzsche: Becoming a Genius* (New York: Free Press, 1991), 183.

2. Friedrich Nietzsche, *Thus Spake Zarathustra*, trans. Walter Kaufmann (New York: Viking, 1966), 14. All other short quotes from Nietzsche are from this edition.

3. George J. Stack, *Nietzsche and Emerson: An Elective Affinity* (Athens: Ohio Univ. Press, 1992), 338.

4. Walter Kaufmann, *Nietzsche: Philosopher, Psychologist, Antichrist*, 3rd ed. (New York: Vintage, 1968), 313–314.

5. Nietzsche, *The Genealogy of Morals*, trans. Walter Kaufmann, excerpted in *Existentialism*, ed. Robert Solomon (New York: Modern Library, 1974), 68–69.

6. Georg Simmel, *Schopenhauer and Nietzsche*, trans. H. Loskandl, D. Weinstein, and M. Weinstein (Univ. of Illinois Press, 1991), 166.

7. M. S. Silk and J. P. Stern, *Nietzsche on Tragedy* (Cambridge, Eng.: Cambridge Univ. Press, 1981), 296.

8. Martin Heidegger, "Who Is Zarathustra?" in *The New Nietzsche*, ed. and trans. David Allison (Cambridge, MA: MIT Press, 1985), 67.

HOUSE AND MORAL LUCK

Jane Dryden

The Problem of Moral Luck

A patient presents with a complicated set of symptoms. The team of doctors comes up with two plausible diagnoses, each with a different treatment. Each treatment will cure the patient if the diagnosis turns out to be correct, but of course, in a pattern familiar to viewers of *House*, either treatment could kill the patient if the diagnosis is wrong. If the doctors are right, they will be praised; if they are wrong, even if they are not punished, they will still regret their actions. The patient's family will be angry at the team if the diagnosis is wrong. The team has killed their loved one, and surely that is cause for blame. Or is it? Is the team really to blame in this case, if they had no real way of knowing which of the two diagnoses would be correct? What if there was some small symptom they missed? Are they now to blame for their negligence, even if other doctors might have missed the same symptom? If they are not blameworthy when they get it wrong, then how do we justify praising them when they get it right?

We don't want to blame someone for something that isn't his fault—something beyond his control. We can call this the Control Principle. But, paradoxically, we blame people more when their actions cause serious harm than when those same actions, through sheer luck, cause no harm at all. For example, a drunk driver who kills someone has done something far worse, we feel, than a drunk driver who does not kill anyone. This paradox—that we are responsible only for what we control, and yet we are also responsible for things beyond our control—is known in philosophy as the problem of "moral luck." It complicates our ideas about how moral responsibility is supposed to work. While consideration of the nature of luck, and the importance of factors beyond our control, has long been a part of moral philosophy, the current discussion of moral luck grew out of two papers written in 1976 by Bernard Williams[1] and Thomas Nagel.[2] Nagel's paper pointed out that the problem of moral luck shows us that there's something strange about our most basic ideas of praise and blame. Nagel writes, "The view that moral luck is paradoxical is not a mistake, ethical or logical, but a perception of one of the ways in which the intuitively acceptable conditions of moral judgment threaten to undermine it all."[3]

Results Are What Matter

It's probably not surprising that given House's dubious attitude toward the usefulness of morality in general (this is, after all, the man who bribed and blackmailed a transplant surgeon into performing a liver transplant!), he is generally not concerned with the finer points of moral judgment. Given that patients' lives are at stake, what matters are results.

In the season one episode "Three Stories," House lectures to a group of medical students and asks them what they would do with a particular snakebite victim who was almost just killed by being given the wrong antivenom. Time is running out for the victim. Do they try giving him another antivenom, hoping it is the right one and knowing the wrong one might indeed kill him this time? Do they search the victim's farm again, hoping to find the snake that bit him so that they can identify the correct antivenom without risking using a wrong one, knowing that the patient may die by the time they find the snake? One of the students notes that choosing the wrong option will probably kill the patient, and House nods. The class ends up split down the middle in their choice. Another one of the students then concludes, horrified, "Half of us killed him and half of us just saved his life." House agrees. A third student begins to protest that they cannot be blamed for killing the patient, thus demonstrating his belief in the Control Principle—since it was beyond their control to know what the correct option would be at the time of their decision, they should not be responsible.

House responds, "I'm sure this goes against everything you've been taught, but right and wrong do exist. Just because you don't know what the right answer is—maybe there's even no way you could know what the right answer is—doesn't make your answer right or even okay. It's much simpler than that. It's just plain wrong." The judge of correctness is outcome. It doesn't matter what their intentions were. The Control Principle is wrong, according to House.

In the season two episode "The Mistake," Chase fails to ask a patient a key question after he is distracted by the news of his father's death, and this failure leads, down the line, to the patient's death. When Chase tries to protest that it is just a little mistake (and thus not very blameworthy), House responds, "Mistakes are as serious as the results they cause." Had the patient not died, the mistake would have been less serious. It would indeed have been a simple failure to ask a particular follow-up question, rather than grounds for a disciplinary hearing and a medical malpractice and negligence suit. The action in either case is the same: failure to ask a question. Because the patient died, however, Chase committed a serious error, and only the mitigating factor of having just learned of his father's death is ultimately able to excuse him, so that all he receives is a week's suspension and a letter in his permanent file.

The idea that unintended or unforeseen consequences of an action determine whether the agent will be in serious trouble or not can be frightening. The kind of moral luck involved here is called *resultant luck*. We can mitigate resultant luck somewhat by attempting to control for as many factors as we can—much as House controls for the probability of his patients' being deceitful by holding "Everybody lies" as a firm rule—but ultimately much is beyond our control. House's team will need to take risks and try treatments that may not work, because ultimately they are expected to do something rather than nothing.

Agent-Regret and Feeling Guilty

Inevitably, some of these risks, and treatments, will not work. What, then, is the appropriate response when an action has unfortunate results that are beyond our control?

Bernard Williams, in a 1976 essay, defines the concept of "agent-regret." Regret in general, as Williams defines it, involves our thinking "something like 'how much better if it had been otherwise.' "[4] Agent-regret is the regret that we feel after some action of ours has led, in some way, to consequences that we wish had been otherwise. Unlike plain regret, which mere spectators or bystanders might feel, agent-regret is tied to our own past actions. Agent-regret is also different from remorse, which is when we feel bad about what we have done and wish we had done otherwise. A feeling of agent-regret can go along perfectly well with feeling that we did the right thing and would do it again, despite our sadness at how things worked out. To make this distinction clearer, consider the example that Williams gives of a driver who, though driving safely, accidentally runs over a child.[5] This driver will probably feel a great deal of regret at this, even if it was not really his fault. Others around the driver will probably attempt to comfort the driver and attempt to make him feel less bad about what had happened, but Williams points out that there would seem to be something *wrong* if the driver was too quickly reassured, if his response was too bland. Because the death of the child was the result of his own agency, his own driving, there is some sort of important connection there; the spectators, for instance, will also regret the death of the child, but not feel that they had anything to do with it. Their regret will not be agent-regret. Had the driver been drunk, or otherwise impaired, while driving, his feelings would be more like remorse for having acted badly.

In the season three episode "House Training," Foreman diagnoses a patient as having cancer and suggests a radiation treatment. After the radiation, it's revealed that the patient actually has an infection, and that due to the radiation's destruction of her immune system, she will die within the day. Most of the latter half of the episode is taken up with Foreman's strong agent-regret over having "killed" the patient (his feelings are probably also heightened by the fact that he and the patient didn't get along very well, ironically arguing over whether she is responsible for her unfortunate life through having made a series of bad decisions).

Chase tries to reassure Foreman by pointing out that "we were all wrong, you know. Even House was wrong." Foreman recognizes this, but it doesn't lessen his regret. Foreman came up with a diagnosis, explained how it fit the symptoms, ran it by the team, and got House's approval (House even calls it "a rad move"). This process is a good one, even though in this instance it not only failed to cure the patient but directly led to her death. It makes sense to feel agent-regret at the outcome and to wish that the team had come up with better answers and better ideas during the differential diagnosis, while at the same time affirming that the process that was followed was the right one.

House also tries to reassure Foreman, in his own way. Recalling that the results are what matter, House suggests that Foreman do whatever he needs to do in order to move on: "Go home, have a few drinks, go to sleep, get up tomorrow, do it all over, only better. If you need absolution, go to a priest. Or give alms to the poor. Whatever ritual comforts you." Continuing to act as a good doctor is more important than feeling a certain amount of guilt for a failed diagnosis, and so Foreman should attempt to reduce any guilt that might impair or cloud his future judgments (indeed, in later episodes, House is worried that Foreman's lingering regret is making him too cautious). If a patient dies despite a doctor's hard work, the doctor must move on. House says that he cannot forgive Foreman, as there is nothing to forgive. Their team saves many patients that other teams would lose, but they will lose patients that other doctors, with different methods, might catch. Death is part of the process. Foreman killed his patient, and he will do it again. As House says to Wilson, "Guilt is irrelevant."[6]

Foreman still feels worthy of blame. When Cameron tries to cheer him up, he says, "I killed a woman. Don't you think it's appropriate I feel like crap for just a little while?" Even though it is statistically inevitable that patients will die as the result of attempted treatments, it still makes sense for Foreman to feel bad. We would probably think less of him if he shrugged off the patient's death easily, just as we would think badly of the driver in the example Williams gives. Foreman's use of the term "appropriate" here echoes Williams's point.

Even House, despite his words to Wilson and Foreman, is (unusually for House) bothered by the team's responsibility in her death, offering to be the one to tell the patient that "we killed her," and frantically trying to figure out the cause of her death: "What did we screw up? What did we miss? I need to know." House's reaction appears cold to Foreman, but his feelings seem to go beyond scientific curiosity. When Wilson asks, "She died of a simple staph infection?" House responds, "That and some bad decisions." While the patient's bad decisions had been an earlier topic of discussion in the episode, the team's "bad decisions" concern House, who does feel some regret.

Agent-Regret and Shrugging It Off

Generally, though, House seems to be more like a driver who doesn't display any agent-regret if he feels something was not his fault. The contemporary philosopher Margaret Walker argues that regardless of one's attitude toward moral luck and agent responsibility, at the very least "there is one thing I think we will find at least faulty if not completely unacceptable: that the agent should *shrug it off*."[7] Consider this example of an unacceptable response:

> It's really too bad about what happened and the damage that's been done, but my involvement was just a happenstance that it was my bad luck to suffer. I admit my negligence (dishonesty, cowardice, opportunism, etc.) and accept such blame as is due these common faults. But it would be totally unfair of you to judge, let alone blame me for unlucky results and situations I didn't totally control and stupid or masochistic of me to let you.[8]

Walker points out that this would strike us as disappointing, even shocking, depending on the nature of the case, and that regardless of the particular details of the agent's exact involvement in the action, "we would think there was something wrong with the agent that went deeper than the original offense.[9]

When Chase, in "The Mistake," refers to the patient simply as "the patient" and protests that "I obviously got the diagnosis wrong. But I did everything by the book. I couldn't have known what was going to happen," Stacy, as the hospital lawyer, warns him that such a reaction isn't going to win over the hospital review committee, since it might make it seem as if he doesn't care about his patients. Since Chase did make a mistake, Williams might consider his feelings to be somewhat closer to remorse than simple agent-regret. However, had the patient recovered, it would have remained a small mistake rather than a serious one, and otherwise Chase did do everything "by the book." Chase's wanting to admit his (slight) negligence but not wanting to be blamed for the (serious) consequence is much like Walker's example.

Similarly, before the patient dies, when House points out to Chase that the patient "could die because you were too lazy to ask one simple question," Chase responds that "She might die because I had the bad luck to spill your damn Vicodin pills." It had originally been Foreman who was supposed to take care of the woman, but due to Chase's clumsiness House peevishly assigned the woman to Chase. Consequently, is it then unfair to judge Chase for the unlucky circumstance of the woman being his patient in the first place? Had it been Foreman in charge, Chase would never have had the opportunity to make the mistake at all. This is often referred to as *antecedent luck*, or luck in circumstances.

How much agent-regret is desirable for doctors who must make life-and-death decisions on a regular basis? It would be bad to be paralyzed by it. As House says of the patient who loses her will in "House Training," "What's life without the ability to make stupid choices?" If a patient's organs are rapidly failing, and test results are unlikely to come back before the patient dies, doctors need to go on the information available at the time, however scanty, and make a decision, whatever the results might ultimately be. When can the doctors in *House* be said to have done enough to reasonably protect themselves from excessive regret?

How Much Is a Doctor Responsible For?

In the season three episode "Half-Wit," Foreman suggests a "risky and invasive" treatment for their patient, and House responds, "That's why God invented the long consent form." While House in general seems to take consent forms lightly (in "House Training," he performs an autopsy before Wilson has gotten the consent form signed; in many other episodes he bullies the patients or their caregivers into signing consent forms), the problem of moral luck might be a reason for him to take the forms more seriously. Rather than being simply a legal formality, they could be a doctor's best defense against the vagaries of moral luck.

The contemporary philosopher Donna Dickenson argues that informed consent ought to be taken seriously on moral, and not just legal, grounds, as "it is the giving of informed consent that stops the probability machine rolling, and that shuts out questions about moral luck and risk for the doctor."[10] Knowing that some outcomes, statistically speaking, will be negative, the doctor cannot constantly be bracing herself against feelings of guilt or remorse if the outcome for a particular patient is bad. Informed consent, provided it is obtained properly, serves to transfer the burden of the responsibility for ill luck from the doctor to the patient. The patient, given a reasonable understanding of the risks, assumes responsibility for the risks, provided that the doctors do not perform negligently. As Dickenson writes, "If a procedure turns out badly, the normally competent physician cannot be held ethically at fault if she has obtained informed consent. To put the matter in deliberately oversimplified terms, she will be unlucky but not evil, and should experience regret but not guilt or remorse."[11] If this is true, then the consent form might indeed seem to be a divine magic bullet.

Of course, this puts all the emphasis on the procedure, rather than the outcome. House regularly appeals to the results of his actions, saying that as long as they end up working, all will be well. House can be seen either as a consequentialist (the outcome of an action is what matters in judging it good or bad) or a paternalist (it is up to the doctor to determine what is in the best interests of the patient, regardless of the patient's own values), or both. As Dickenson points out, the "They'll thank you afterwards" argument "can be extremely tempting to clinicians."[12] The problem with this is that if House fails, he is left utterly undefended, ethically. This might not matter to House, but it matters to those around him, and to us, the viewers. Overriding consent or the standards of openness involved in gaining consent, even if the recommended treatment seems to be in the best interests of the patient, is problematic not just for violating a standard of care, but also for the problem of resultant luck: sure, everything is fine if it works (which things usually do for House), but there is no way of knowing for sure that it will. Even though, as Cuddy points out to Foreman in "Deception," House "gets lucky a lot," it still doesn't alter the risks involved in what he's doing.

If the basis for judgment is consequentialist, then bad results mean that the doctor has done something wrong and is blameworthy. Similarly for paternalism; if the results are not in the best interests of the patient, then there is no other defense for them. Dickenson argues that these are thus both problematic. For her, the correct option is that "the doctor's responsibility is not necessarily to get the outcome right, but to proceed in the correct fashion. . . . an absolutist interpretation of consent protects both doctor and patient: the doctor from moral luck, and the patient from invasion of autonomy."[13]

Of course, the problem with informed consent is that it is notoriously tricky to determine what "reasonable standards" are in disclosing the risks to the patient. In addition to this, what happens if the patient is unable to consent, and proxies are either unavailable or illegal (as they are under English law)?[14]

For example, the patient that Foreman "kills" in "House Training" has trouble making decisions. The episode opens with her suffering an attack of abulia (inability to decide, generally due to some form of brain damage), and another attack occurs as House is getting her to sign the consent form. Due to the attack, she can't decide whether or not to sign it. After she loses consciousness, House tells the nurses that she will want to sign the consent form as soon as she wakes up. Further, even when House was giving her the list of risks, he quickly changed the subject to asking her why she didn't like Foreman, rather than giving her time to process and consider the risks. This is hardly a case of thoughtful, reasoned consent. We do not see her when she signs the consent form, but it is unlikely that she is in any position to refuse.

Might the dubious consent be at all related to Foreman's strong agent-regret and even remorse over her death? Had Foreman sought the consent himself, might he feel differently about the outcome? More resigned to it? If the patient had more time to think about the effects of the radiation, and more time to discuss it with her doctors, might she have reacted differently to being told of their mistake in her diagnosis?

The Problem of Purity

Of course, it could be that moral luck is a problem only if we expect moral responsibility to be simple, a matter of black and white. If what we are aiming for is moral purity, in other words, clear-cut judgments about who is guilty and who is innocent, or clear-cut demarcations about what we are and are not responsible for, then moral luck muddies the water. If purity is not important to us, though, then moral luck might simply be a reminder that life isn't simple. According to Walker, it makes more sense to make moral assessments of persons in terms of their actions, rather than considering the actions themselves in isolation. When we consider the context of the whole person, much that appears tricky about moral luck seems to abate. It makes a difference to us, and it seems that it *should* make a difference, whether a speeding driver who causes an injury is speeding in order to tend to a family emergency or whether the driver is drunk and speeding for fun. Finding out that Chase was distracted in "The Mistake" because of his father's death (rather than being hungover or lazy) helps us to refrain from judging him as callous and negligent. The whole episode is set up to play with the difference in our responses to Chase's mistake: for most of the episode, we think he was in fact being lazy or careless. We find out only at the end that it was his father's death that distracted him, and our reaction to this discovery highlights the factors we instinctively use in praising and blaming. After all, "the agent is not a self-sufficient rational will fully expressed in each episode of choice, but is a history of choices and (witting or unwitting) concessions for which episodes are meaningful in terms of much larger stretches, ongoing themes, constitutive or passing projects, up to and including an entire life."[15] We know the nature of Chase's relationship with his father. Chase's distraction doesn't mean he isn't responsible for his patient's death. But it does help us to make a concession for him in this case.

Further, we cannot simply choose what we are going to take responsibility for and what we are not. Just as we expect the faultless driver to feel some sort of regret for killing a child, Walker suggests that "responsibilities outrun control."[16] The larger context of our lives requires us take to responsibility for many events and outcomes that we would not have chosen. This is part of what it is to be human, and the reason that we praise those whose grace and integrity allow them to deal with events and outcomes well. If this is true, then moral luck does not undermine human moral agency, but rather offers it more opportunities in which to practice different virtues.

Certainly *House* would be the wrong show from which to expect too much moral purity. A consideration of the problems involved in moral luck shows us that maybe we shouldn't even try. Rather than thinking that moral responsibility means having control over all of our actions and their consequences, we should recognize the large degree to which actions and consequences are beyond our control. House teaches us that in the midst of this uncertainty, we must have the confidence to act when not to act is almost certainly fatal. We must do the best we can, and be realistically prepared to accept, and take responsibility for, dire consequences.

NOTES

1. Bernard Williams, "Moral Luck," *Moral Luck: Philosophical Papers 1973–1980* (Cambridge: Cambridge Univ. Press, 1981). Reprinted from *Proceedings of the Aristotelian Society*, supplementary vol. 50 (1976).

2. Thomas Nagel, "Moral Luck," in *Mortal Questions* (New York: Cambridge Univ. Press, 1979). Reprinted from *Proceedings of the Aristotelian Society*, supplementary vol. 50 (1976).

3. Ibid., 27.

4. Williams, "Moral Luck," 27.

5. Ibid., 28.

6. Of course, the fact that House's own emotions do not always conform to his beliefs is highlighted by the fact that shortly after uttering this, he reveals that he has taken in Wilson's old dog, out of some sort of sense of guilt induced by Wilson's ex-wife.

7. Margaret Urban Walker, "The Virtues of Impure Agency," in *Moral Luck*, ed. Daniel Statman (Albany: State Univ. of New York Press, 1993), 240.

8. Ibid.

9. Ibid.

10. Donna Dickenson, *Risk and Luck in Medical Ethics* (Cambridge: Polity Press, 2003), 65. I will not attempt to cover the legal aspects of informed consent, as that would take much more space than I have here.

11. Ibid., 84.

12. Ibid., 78.

13. Ibid., 84–85.

14. Ibid., 157.

15. Margaret Walker (Coyne), "Moral Luck?", *Journal of Value Inquiry* 19, no.4 (1985): 322–323.

16. Walker, *Moral Luck*, 241.

PART TWO

"WELCOME TO THE END OF THE THOUGHT PROCESS": HOUSE'S LOGIC AND METHOD

THE LOGIC OF GUESSWORK IN SHERLOCK HOLMES AND *HOUSE*

Jerold J. Abrams

No, no: I never guess. It is a shocking habit—
destructive to the logical faculty.

> — Sherlock Holmes, in *The Sign of Four*[1]

The Game's Afoot

The name Dr. Gregory House, M.D., combines three of Sir Arthur Conan Doyle's famous fictional detectives: Sherlock Holmes, John Watson, and Tobias Gregson. The last name *House* is a synonym for home, which is how Holmes pronounces his name (though with an "s" at the end). The medical initials in House's name, "Dr." and "M.D.," are also those of Dr. Watson, Holmes's trusted friend and assistant. But then Watson and Holmes are, in turn, also based on two real-life medical doctors. Conan Doyle was a practicing physician in his own right, and he looked up with awe, as Watson looks up to Holmes, to Dr. Joseph Bell, M.D., of the Royal Infirmary of Edinburgh, whose character, profile, and seemingly magical powers of detection became those of Holmes.[2] House's first name, Gregory, is a little harder to spot, but it's right there in the first Holmes adventure, *A Study in Scarlet*, in the form of Scotland Yard detective Tobias Gregson. Holmes tells Watson that Gregson is "the smartest of the Scotland Yarders," essentially "the pick of a bad lot."[3] Gregson brings Holmes his hardest cases, the ones he can't solve, just as Cuddy brings her hardest cases to House when no one else at Princeton-Plainsboro Teaching Hospital has even a clue. Gregson's and Watson's intellectual limitations are important because they reflect the reader's dumbfoundedness about Holmes. They provide the perspective we need on the genius we're not. Likewise, we could hardly sympathize, let alone identify, with the brilliant House without all his personal and physical difficulties. They humanize him, just as Watson and Gregson humanize Holmes.

House and Holmes

House is, however, not just based on the character of Holmes. In a sense, he actually *is* Holmes, existing somehow between two parallel universes: one in the present at Princeton-Plainsboro, the other in the past at No. 221B Baker Street in London. House even talks like Holmes. For example, looking at a sick patient, House asks, "What are the suspects?" ("Pilot"), and once the disease is diagnosed, he proudly declares, "I solved the case" ("Pilot"). Getting from suspects to whodunit, House looks at patients as frauds and liars, just as Holmes looks at clients. Sick as they are, they're always in the way, so House works around them. He breaks into their homes, steals their belongings, rummages through their drawers—anything to gather clues; again, same as Holmes.[4]

And like Holmes, too, House always has help: a team of young doctors at his beck and call. These are House's Watsons: Cameron, Foreman, and Chase, each with a different specialization. They are not, however, friends or confidants to House, as Watson is to Holmes. That role is reserved for House's fourth Watson, his peer Dr. James Wilson, who shares Watson's initials: "Dr. J. W., M.D." Wilson also lives with House for a time, just as Watson and Holmes share rooms on Baker Street. Together these four neo-Watsons engage House with the questions we, the viewers, have about the case, just as Watson engages Holmes on the progress of the case. They are how we get close to a genius. Otherwise, we would have no way in. House and Holmes are not open people. They're loners, unmarried, unconnected; they care little for others, and can be curt and insulting even to their assistants. In fact, all they really care about is solving the case. They live for the rush of investigation, nothing else. Everything is geared toward that end: their academic pursuits, their musical interests, their seeming recreational activities, even their drug habits—all of it is a means to the final end of knowing whodunit.

House's Logic

Among their parallels, the most important is methodology. Both Holmes and House conceive their logics as deductive, and both are quite wrong![5] All great fictional detectives mistake their methods as deductive, and most, like Holmes, simply scoff at guesswork: "I never guess." But Holmes *does* guess (*The Sign of Three*),[6] as do all detectives and all medical diagnosticians. House also mistakes his method as deduction: "Figuring requires deductive reasoning" ("Acceptance"); and: "I mean, because he said that it hurt and I should have deduced that meant it was sore" ("Occam's Razor"). If House and Holmes, however, truly did use deduction, then their inferences would be entirely error-free and guesswork-free, because in deduction, if the premises are true, then the conclusion *must* be true. For example, given two true premises, "All doctors make mistakes" and "House is a doctor," we know with certainty our conclusion: "House makes mistakes." We know our conclusion with certainty because we know something about all doctors: namely, that they make mistakes. There's no conjecture or probability about it. But none of Holmes's inferences follow with necessity. They're all conjectural. They're very *good* conjectures, but conjectures just the same.

By contrast, House quite interestingly—while he certainly mistakes his method as deduction—never denies an element of guesswork within his method, despite regular attacks from Cuddy, as in this example from "Pilot":

Cuddy: You don't prescribe medicine based on guesses. At least we don't since Tuskegee and Mengele.

House: You're comparing me to a Nazi. Nice.

Cuddy: I'm stopping the treatment.

Cuddy is actually doubly wrong here. She's wrong about doctors prescribing medicine on guesses; they do, all the time. She's also wrong about the equation of unethical medicine with lack of deductive validity. All medicine, ethical or unethical, and all science, for that matter, is ultimately a matter of conjecture. House knows all this, and he knows, too, that what *really* bothers Cuddy is the lack of proof in House's method. But House accepts this lack of proof in his inferences as the essence of medicine—again, despite his mistaken self-assessment of a *deductive* method, as in this exchange from "Pilot":

House: There's never any proof. Five different doctors come up with five different diagnoses based on the same evidence.

Cuddy: You don't have *any* evidence. And nobody knows anything, huh? And how is it you always think you're right?

House: I don't. I just find it hard to operate on the opposite assumption. And why are you so afraid of making a mistake?

Championing a method riddled with error, House appears almost opposite Holmes, who brags to Watson his method is error-free: "There's no room for a mistake."[7] Holmes backs it up, too: he's virtually always correct, so his successes just further fuel his overconfidence, but they shouldn't, because—for all his success—every single case is fraught with a mistaken understanding of methodology. House, however, never makes this mistake about making mistakes. He makes them all the time, but he knows making them only gets him closer to the truth. He understands that the fallibility of his guesswork logic is essential to his method—and House, at least in this respect, is superior to his alter ego Holmes.

On the other hand, Holmes, to his credit, spends far more time in self-analysis. So we know more about his method, which means we have more to criticize as well as praise, while House keeps his methodological cards closer to the vest, much to our chagrin. We'd like to hear more from this Holmesian master about what it is he thinks he's doing, especially when it comes to logic and reason, and the reading of clues. We'd like to hear something like this:

Most people, if you describe a train of events to them, will tell you what the result would be. They can put those events together in their minds, and argue from them that something will come to pass. There are few people, however, who, if you told them a result, would be able to evolve from their own inner consciousness what the steps were which led up to that result. This power is what I mean when I talk of reasoning backward, or analytically.[8]

Passages like this one reveal something important about Holmes. He may be wrong about deduction, wrong about error, and wrong about guesswork. But his analysis of deduction, or what he calls "reasoning backward," looks strangely familiar, and exactly like guesswork. We begin with a result in the present, an effect, and then track the development of that effect back in time along a continuum looking for a cause. Often we run into error because multiple causes could explain a single effect, and there's just no *deducing* the right one. It has to be a guess, and it's achieved exactly the way Holmes says it is.

The formal version of "reasoning backwards" was developed by the American philosopher and originator of "pragmatism" Charles S. Peirce (1839–1914), who called it "abduction" and defined it—contra Holmes—precisely as the logic of guesswork: "abduction is, after all, nothing but guessing."[9] It looks like this:

Abduction
The surprising fact, C, is observed;
But if A were true, C would be a matter of course;
Hence, there is reason to suspect that A is true.[10]

There are three steps in abduction. First, the surprise, an anomaly; medicine runs on them, as House points out: "Doctors love anomalies" ("Acceptance").[11] Faced with the anomaly, House seeks to explain its causal source by means of a rule that would render that anomaly a matter of course. What possible pattern in nature, or culture, would cause this result? Reasoning backward in time, from effects to causes and back again, House selects the most likely cause, and then orders the tests to see if he's right. Of course, again, it's only a guess, a conjecture. And he could be wrong. But even if he's wrong, still, at least then he has new information and can now make a better abduction.

Part of the reason abduction runs into error so often, from a logical point of view, is that it's invalid, meaning there's no sure way of saying if our conclusion will be true, even if our premises are true. So, for example, we could begin with a surprising result and formulate a pretty good rule that explains that result, but we could easily be wrong all the same. The conclusion will never (and can never) follow from the premises with necessity. But then again, abduction doesn't pretend to demonstrate once and for all that a conclusion simply must be the case. All an abduction provides is a reasonable hypothesis as to what *could* be the case. It's more than a shot in the dark, but sometimes not much more.

House's Abductions

In any given episode, House has two cases going at once: one is a clinical walk-in, the other is chosen for its challenge. These two kinds of cases also correspond to two kinds of abduction, as Umberto Eco defines them: overcoded and undercoded.[12] The clinical walk-ins require overcoded abductions: they're simple and easy. A man wonders why his skin is orange, and House knows right away, and he knows other things, too, as revealed in this exchange from "Pilot":

> House: Unfortunately you have a deeper problem. Your wife is having an affair.
>
> Man: What?
>
> House: You're orange, you moron. It's one thing for *you* not to notice. But if your wife hasn't picked up on the fact that her husband has changed color, she's just not paying attention. By the way, do you consume just a ridiculous amount of carrots and megadose vitamins?

[Man nods.] Carrots turn you yellow, the niacin turns you red. Find some finger paint and do the math. And get a good lawyer.

House begins with the first result: a man is orange. But if the man ate lots of carrots and megadose vitamins containing niacin, then he would turn orange. Therefore, he probably eats carrots and niacin. A second result emerges. No one else has noticed the change in color, and the man wears a wedding ring. But if his wife were having an affair, then that would explain her lack of interest in him—and indeed later we see she was having an affair.

The more interesting cases, however, are those House takes by choice and that require undercoded abductions. After the symptoms are catalogued, House gathers his team. One by one they generate possibilities to explain the anomalies. House writes these on a wipe board. Some are eliminated as too improbable, others for inconsistency with the symptoms. Gradually the possible diagnoses are reduced to a few. These are then organized hierarchically according to likelihood and efficiency of testing. The cycle of testing and abduction continues until the right diagnosis is in hand, and House has solved the case.

Developing the final undercoded abduction, however, is often incredibly difficult, and House must rely on his very creative imagination in order to solve the case. In particular, neo–Sherlock Holmes that he is, House thinks of diseases metaphorically as criminals in order to see the problem afresh, as we observe in "Autopsy":

House: The tumor is Afghanistan. The clot is Buffalo. Does that need more explanation? Okay. The tumor is Al-Qaeda, the big bad guy with brains. We went in and wiped it out, but it had already sent out a splinter cell, a small team of low-level terrorists, quietly living in some suburb of Buffalo, waiting to kill us all.

Foreman: Whoa, whoa, whoa. Are you trying to say that the tumor threw a clot before we removed it?

House: It was an excellent metaphor. Angio her brain before this clot straps on an explosive vest.

The abduction works like this. After removing a tumor, symptoms of the tumor persist. But if the tumor, just prior to being removed, threw a microscopic terrorist clot, then that clot could cause the symptoms in question and would explain the anomaly.[13]

Musement and Abduction

House's team stands by and watches him in near disbelief. They think he's mad. They're right: he is, and he shares this with Holmes as well. Holmes is actually doubly mad. His mind is strongly divided, as though there were two Sherlock Holmeses inside him. One of these is mad with energy and intensity when tracking clues: "'Come, Watson, come!' he cried. 'The game is afoot. Not a word! Into your clothes and come!'"[14] The other Holmes is the opposite: not mad with energy, but contemplative, dreamy, even hallucinatory. Watson describes these two sides:

> In his singular character the dual nature alternately asserted itself, and his extreme exactness and astute-ness represented, as I have often thought, the reaction against the poetic and contemplative mood which occa-sionally predominated in him. The swing of his nature took him from extreme languor to devouring energy.[15]

At first, Watson doesn't quite understand what's going on with the strange swing of Holmes's mind. But gradually he learns this zombielike trance is an essential and prior step to solving any very difficult case. After assimilating clues in the hunt, Holmes will retreat to his rooms on Baker Street and sink deeply into his armchair, listening to music, with "a dreamy, vacant expression in his eyes."[16]

Peirce calls this pre-abductive dream state "musement" and defines it as the "pure play" of the imagination. After all the clues have been gathered, the detective must pull back from the case, relax his eyes, and retreat into his imagination. There, wild visions and diagrammatic scenarios of causality flash by. All the results and all the possible rules are shuffled about, as the detective looks for the perfect fit.[17]

Likewise with House: he, too, has two sides, though they are not nearly as extreme as those of Holmes. At one moment, House is mad with energy, standing before the wipe board with all the various possible diagnoses written before his team, yelling at Cameron and Chase and Foreman, yelling at Cuddy, and even swatting them with his cane. But then he'll stop, almost all of a sudden, and retreat back to his office, kick back, and enter the Holmesian musement state, gently waving his hand back and forth, drifting in a logical delirium as he listens to John Henry Giles's (Harry J. Lennix) jazz recording, as he did in the episode "DNR." This scene in House was virtually taken right out of Conan Doyle's "The Red-Headed League":

> All afternoon he sat in the stalls wrapped in the most perfect happiness, gently waving his long, thin fingers in time to the music, while his gently smiling face and his languid, dreamy eyes were as unlike those of Holmes, the sleuthhound, Holmes the relentless, keen-witted, ready-handed criminal agent, as it was possible to conceive.[18]

Entering either the musement state or the "sleuthhound" state, Holmes was also known to rely on intoxicating drugs. House's drug of choice is Vicodin, partly because it kills pain and allows him to focus on the details of the case, but also for its euphoric and relaxing, contemplative effects; in other words, because it enhances the musement state and allows him to form better undercoded abductions.[19]

House vs. Moriarty

In one particular case, however, House is truly stumped. He finds himself not only alienated from his team, but even his own mind. He's been shot twice point-blank in his office by a man named Moriarty ("No Reason").[20] The name is important because it's also the name of Holmes's archnemesis, Professor James Moriarty, who appears in "The Final Problem" and *The Valley of Fear*. A true criminal mastermind, Moriarty is every bit Holmes's equal in genius: "I had at last met an antagonist who was my intellectual equal."[21] And Holmes has nothing but the utmost respect for Moriarty's powers:

> He is the Napoleon of crime, Watson. He is the orga-
> nizer of half that is evil and of nearly all that is unde-
> tected in this great city. He is a genius, a philosopher,
> an abstract thinker. He has a brain of the first order. He
> sits motionless, like a spider in the centre of its web, but
> that web has a thousand radiations, and he knows well
> every quiver of each of them.[22]

Having bested so many of London's criminals, Holmes now finds himself at the very center of the web of crime, opposing the leader of all the criminals, and so it is a fitting ending when, after so many great adventures, Moriarty finally kills Holmes. But the death is an illusion. For in "The Adventure of the Empty House," Holmes miraculously returns, much to Watson's amazement: " 'Holmes!' I cried. 'Is it really you? Can it indeed be that you are alive? Is it possible that you succeeded in climbing out of that awful abyss?' "[23]

This cycle of murder and rebirth is imitated in "No Reason," after Moriarty shoots House and leaves him for dead. House wakes up near death, in a hospital bed next to Moriarty, who has also been shot, by security guards. Always the arrogant diagnostician, House thinks he's already solved his own case: he knows why Moriarty did it. But House is wrong. His diagnostics are off, and Moriarty can see right through him as House struggles to talk with his team. He's slower after the shooting. Something happened to his mind. Usually he has to lead his team through the case, but this time they're off and testing before House is done reasoning. Even Chase, the slowest of the three, is too fast, too good. House is disturbed, but Moriarty is not surprised, and he delights in taunting the so-called master: "Maybe he knew the answer because the question wasn't nearly as tricky as you thought. Maybe he's not getting smarter. Maybe you're getting dumber" ("No Reason").

But even if House is slower, he knows Moriarty knows too much. He knows, too, the time continuum seems a little broken. And all of a sudden, he can walk without a cane and his leg pain is gone. Steadily the anomalies build up around him, and House makes the abduction that he is hallucinating. Moriarty doesn't really exist. He's inside of House's mind. Chase isn't really brilliant, and his leg isn't really better. But with his new abduction in hand, House is now struck with a further result: he cannot break free of the hallucination by will alone. But if he were to attack his own unconscious mind, which is producing the hallucination, then that might break the spell. In order to achieve a sufficiently graphic and effective attack on his mind, House murders his own patient in cold blood.

In murdering his patient, House uses what Lorenzo Magnani calls "manipulative abduction": "manipulating observations to get new data, and 'actively' building experiments."[24] And here, too, House is Holmes's descendant. For, just before their first meeting, Watson learns Holmes has been beating dead bodies to coax clues. Watson's old friend Stamford says: "When it comes to beating the subjects in the dissecting-rooms with a stick, it is certainly taking rather a bizarre shape."

Watson can barely believe it. But Stamford assures him: "Yes, to verify how far bruises may be produced after death. I saw him at it with my own eyes."[25]

Likewise House will often give a patient a mix of medicines, or cause her undue stress, in order to reveal other symptoms. And now he must do the same on himself: he must manipulate his own mind to derive new data. And it works. House suddenly awakes to find himself being wheeled into the emergency room, barely conscious, having just been shot. House has, by this point, made three abductions: that he is hallucinating, that breaking his ultimate oath will break his hallucination, and that he may yet cure his leg pain. Earlier in his hallucination, reading his chart, he found that ketamine was administered, and he demanded an explanation from Cuddy, who provided it: "There's a clinic in Germany. They've been treating chronic pain by inducing comas and letting the mind basically reboot itself" ("No Reason"). That explained his newly painless leg (but not the sudden muscular development). House realizes that he was no more talking to Cuddy than to Moriarty. He was talking to himself, and even unconscious, he was working out an abduction for a cure to his pain. Barely conscious, House utters only one sentence: "Tell Cuddy, I want ketamine" ("No Reason").

It's Elementary, My Dear Cameron

Of all the lines ever quoted from Sherlock Holmes, the most famous is certainly this one: "It's elementary, my dear Watson." Everyone knows it. The problem is, Holmes never said it.[26] Still, he might as well have, given his habit of regularly insulting the slow-witted Watson. House does the same with his team. But he is perhaps most cruel to Cameron, who loves him. They have dinner once, and Cameron wants to talk. It's just so simple, she thinks: they can be together, if only he'd try.

After all, she knows that on some level he wants her. But it's just as clear to House that they can't be together. So, instead of romantic conversation, House ever-the-sleuth delivers his diagnosis, callous and direct, as though Cameron were laid out on a hospital bed, rather than dressed to the nines for an intimate evening. She is broken, and she falls in love with broken men; she treats them as projects to work on. Now she's chosen him because he's broken, too.

As she hears her diagnosis, she knows it's true. But what she doesn't know, and what House doesn't seem to know either, is *why* exactly he's broken. It's not lack of love or leg pain or even drug addiction. These are symptoms, not causes, and besides, House was House before the infarction (muscle death) in his right leg, the same guy he's always been. His illness, rather, is logical: or, abductive, to be more precise; and it's progressive and degenerative. The better House gets rationally, the worse he gets psychologically. The abductions become faster, his perception more fine-tuned. This one overcoded, that one undercoded, two at once, all day long: inferences about his team and their problems, Cuddy, a rat, a guy in the park, anything and anyone, God, and the human condition. He just can't stop; and as many Vicodins he tosses back, they're no relief from his magnificent gifts. The true tragedy of House is abductive reason run amok in the mind of a mad genius who, like all mad geniuses, must ultimately self-destruct.

NOTES

1. Sir Arthur Conan Doyle, *The Complete Sherlock Holmes* (New York: Barnes and Noble Books, 1992), 93.

2. Christopher Morley, "In Memoriam," in *The Complete Sherlock Holmes*, 8; and Thomas Sebeok and Jean Umiker-Sebeok, " 'You Know My Method': A Juxtaposition of Charles S. Peirce and Sherlock Holmes," in *The Sign of Three: Dupin, Holmes, Peirce*, ed. Umberto Eco and Thomas Sebeok (Bloomington: Indiana Univ. Press, 1983), 30–31.

3. Doyle, *A Study in Scarlet*, in *The Complete Sherlock Holmes*, 26–27.

4. It's worth noting here that House's knowledge of chemistry, like that of a doctor's, is "profound," while his knowledge of anatomy is "accurate, but unsystematic" (*A Study in Scarlet*, 22).

5. A further interesting parallel is the common use of a cane. House uses one to support a bad leg. Holmes uses one, too (but rarely). In "The Adventure of the Speckled Band," Watson says: "The instant that we heard it, Holmes sprang from the bed, struck a match, and lashed furiously with his cane at the bell-pull" (Doyle, *The Complete Sherlock Holmes*, 271). And in "The Red-Headed League," Watson says: "The light flashed upon the barrel of a revolver, but Holmes's hunting crop came down on the man's wrist, and the pistol clinked upon the stone floor" (Doyle, *The Complete Sherlock Holmes*, 189). A hunting crop is a kind of cane.

6. Eco and Sebeok, eds., *The Sign of Three*; see especially Sebeok and Jean Umiker-Sebeok, "'You Know My Method': A Juxtaposition of Charles S. Peirce and Sherlock Holmes," 11–54.

7. Doyle, *A Study in Scarlet*, 32.

8. Ibid., 83–84.

9. Charles S. Peirce, "On the Logic of Drawing History from Ancient Documents," in *The Essential Peirce: Selected Philosophical Writings*, vol. 2 (1893–1913), ed. the Peirce Edition Project (Bloomington: Indiana Univ. Press, 1998), 107.

10. Peirce, "Pragmatism as the Logic of Abduction," in *The Essential Peirce*, vol. 2, 231.

11. Often in medicine, and certainly on *House*, these anomalies are produced by chance events.

12. Eco and Sebeok, eds. *The Sign of Three*, 206–207.

13. Executive producer David Shore also notes the importance of House's use of metaphor on the DVD Commentary for "Autopsy": "These metaphors are actually kind of crucial to the show." I am very grateful to Bill Irwin for discussion of House's use of metaphors.

14. Doyle, *The Adventure of the Abbey Grange*, in *The Complete Sherlock Holmes*, 636.

15. Doyle, "The Red-Headed League," 183.

16. Doyle, *A Study in Scarlet*, 20.

17. Peirce writes that in musement "those problems that at first blush appear utterly insoluble receive, in that very circumstance,—as Edgar Poe remarked in his 'The Murders in the Rue Morgue,'—their smoothly-fitting keys. This particularly adapts them to the Play of Musement" ("A Neglected Argument for the Reality of God," in *The Essential Peirce*, vol. 2, 437). Note further that Sherlock Holmes was based on Edgar Allan Poe's character C. Auguste Dupin, who also relies on the musement state to solve cases.

18. Doyle, "The Red-Headed League," 184. House also plays the piano ("The Socratic Method," "Damned If You Do, Damned If You Don't"), just as Holmes plays the violin to get in the musement mood.

19. House also keeps a syringe at home for morphine.

20. David Shore reveals and discusses the name and character of Moriarty on the DVD Commentary to "No Reason."

21. Doyle, "The Final Problem," in *The Complete Sherlock Holmes*, 471.

22. Ibid.

23. Ibid., 487.

24. Lorenzo Magnani, *Abduction, Reason, and Science: Processes of Discovery and Explanation* (New York: Kluwer Academic/Plenum Publishers, 2001), 64.

25. Doyle, *A Study in Scarlet*, 17.

26. Sebeok and Umiker-Sebeok, "'You Know My Method,'" 49n7.

IT EXPLAINS EVERYTHING!

Barbara Anne Stock

Some things just happen for no reason, right? Not according to Gregory House. The surly doctor endorses a view that philosophers call the Principle of Sufficient Reason (PSR, for short), which states that there is a rational explanation for every event. You might not *know* what the true explanation is, but there always *is* one. Of course, even supposing that a particular event or situation does have an explanation, one still needs to figure out what that explanation is. House, for the most part, does this by employing standard scientific methods: he identifies hypotheses that match the patient's symptoms (for example, "it's lupus," "it's vasculitis"), then tests these hypotheses to discern which is correct. Unfortunately, the tests are often inconclusive. As we'll see, when that happens, House applies more controversial criteria for deciding which explanation to prefer.

The Principle of Sufficient Reason

Gottfried Wilhelm Leibniz, a seventeenth-century German philosopher, wrote, "Nothing takes place without sufficient reason, that is . . . nothing happens without it being possible for someone who knows enough things to give a reason sufficient to determine why it is so and not otherwise."[1] Later Leibniz added that we often do not know these reasons. This principle of sufficient reason (PSR) flatly rejects the possibility of random or unexplainable events. Even if we are not aware of the reason behind a particular event, it is nevertheless true that there is a reason that fully explains why the event took place. House echoes this principle in the following exchange with Wilson from "Damned If You Do":

> Wilson: I want you to accept that sometimes patients die against all reason. Sometimes they get better against all reason.
>
> House: No, they don't. We just don't know the reason.

In addition to verbally assenting to the PSR, House shows his commitment to it through his behavior. He is not satisfied with partial answers or theories that sort of explain most of the symptoms. Whether it means trolling the waiting room for the carrier who spread a virus (in "Maternity") or rummaging through the hospital's supply of colchicine to find pills that might have been mistaken for cough medicine (in "Occam's Razor"), he is convinced that there is a complete answer out there and he is determined to find it. And, of course, he has no patience for conditions that other doctors term idiopathic (of unknown origin): "Idiopathic, from the Latin meaning we're idiots 'cause we can't figure out what's causing it" ("Role Model").

But what kinds of reasons are appropriate? Often when people say things like "Everything happens for a reason," they have particularly deep or meaningful reasons in mind. For example, in "Damned If You Do," when Sister Augustine says, "If I break my leg, I believe it happened for a reason," the reason she cites is God's will. Someone who believes in fate or karma might turn to these as reasons. House would agree that the break happened for a reason, but he would offer medical reasons, such as osteoporosis weakening the bone, or reasons from physics, such as the force of a hard object impacting the affected body part. So clearly House's acceptance of the PSR does not commit him to believing in supernatural explanations or any kind of higher meaning behind events. There is always a reason . . . a scientifically respectable one, that is.

Is the Principle of Sufficient Reason true? It seems to make sense in everyday life. In "Top Secret," House dreams about a marine, then immediately is handed the marine's file as a new patient. Imagine if, instead of speculating about House's daddy issues and discussing the Village People, Wilson had said, "Get over it! It's just a coincidence!" That wouldn't satisfy House, or the audience. There must be some explanation for this odd turn of events. Even things that seem random have reasons. When you flip a coin and it lands heads-up, that might at first seem random. But if one could really know all the facts (the exact position of the coin before you flipped it, the force with which your thumb pivoted it, the strength and direction of air currents, and so on), these facts would explain why the coin landed as it did. Suppose three people are in a room with a sick person; one catches the disease, the other two do not. Again, that might at first appear to be a matter of luck, but if we could see the situation through the molecular level "House-Camera" we would see that the path of the disease is determined and explained by physical laws.

The most serious challenge to the PSR comes from considering things at an even smaller level: the subatomic level. A widely held interpretation of quantum physics asserts that at the subatomic level causality is indeterministic, which means that past events create a certain probability that a future event will follow, but they do not *determine* that the event will happen. For example, the probability may be 50 percent that a radioactive compound will release a subatomic particle within a certain period of time. Suppose that, in fact, it does release a particle. What is the reason or explanation for why it did so at that time? There is none. It happened, but it could just as easily not have happened. Hence, the PSR is wrong. A secondary challenge points out that even if the PSR were true, there is no way we could prove it. Perhaps one can know that within one's own experience there has always been an explanation for everything that has happened. But that does not prove that nothing *ever* happens without a reason.

If House held out against these challenges, he would be in good company. Albert Einstein never accepted the indeterministic interpretation of quantum physics, famously retorting that God does not play dice with the universe. But unless Stephen Hawking turns up as the patient-of-the-week, House need not bother trying to defend the *truth* of the PSR. Instead, he can justify it as pragmatically valuable. Consider the following exchange, which took place in "DNR" after the patient surprised the team by regaining sensation in his legs:

> House: He now has feeling all the way up to the calf. This is the way medicine evolved. Patients sometimes get better. You have no idea why, but unless you give a reason they won't pay you. Anybody notice if there's a full moon?
>
> Cameron: You're saying he just spontaneously got better?
>
> House: No, I'm saying let's rule out the lunar god and go from there.

Medicine, as a science, progresses by doctors assuming that there are reasons behind their patients' symptoms. If, upon seeing their patient's improvement, the team had responded, "Cool. He's getting better. Don't want to mess with that! Let's go home," there would be no advancement of knowledge. If, on the other hand, they see the improvement as something in need of explanation, that puts them in a better position to find the explanation, should there be one, and thus advance medical knowledge.

Another reason to defend House's application of the PSR, though not the PSR itself, comes from contemporary philosopher Peter van Inwagen, who proposes the following test for which events require explanation:

> Suppose there is a certain fact that has no known explanation; suppose that one can think of a possible explanation of that fact, an explanation that (if only it were true) would be a very good explanation; then it is wrong to say that that event stands in no more need of an explanation than an otherwise similar event for which no explanation is available.[2]

In other words, if you can come up with a very good explanation for something, then it is not reasonable to maintain that no explanation is necessary. Note that just because you come up with an explanation, that does not imply that *your* explanation is true, only that there is probably *some* explanation for the phenomenon. Although van Inwagen's criterion does not guarantee that all events will admit to explanation, it does justify House's assumption that the events he studies—patients' symptoms—require explanation, as long as he can identify some possible explanations (diseases) that would account for them.

Finding the Right Explanation

Let's suppose, then, with House, that symptoms and changes in symptoms don't just happen, that there is always a reason or explanation behind them. How does one determine what the correct explanation is? House starts out with "Differential diagnosis, people!"—that is, brainstorming possible explanations that might fit the symptoms. The possible diagnoses that survive the initial House-shoots-down-his-fellows'-ideas phase become hypotheses. Hypotheses generate predictions (such as "If it's an infection, her white blood cell count will be elevated"), which can then be tested either by diagnostic procedures or by implementing treatments and seeing how the patient responds. On the basis of the test results, hypotheses can be eliminated or revised until eventually the team arrives at the correct answer.

Chapter 5 in this book is devoted to this method, sometimes called "abductive reasoning," so we won't go into further detail here. Instead, let's discuss what happens when House cannot reach the desired conclusion using this method alone, and must instead add more controversial criteria for deciding which diagnosis is more promising. For example, suppose at the "differential diagnosis" stage there are hundreds of possible explanations, and House's team can't test them all. This can occur when the only symptoms are nonspecific, such as the autistic boy's screaming in "Lines in the Sand." Or suppose, as often happens, the available tests require too much time, or are inconclusive, or the intervention that would confirm one diagnosis would be fatal if that diagnosis is incorrect. In these and other scenarios, House and his team are left with several possible explanations for the patient's symptoms, all of which are consistent with the evidence available. What other factors can be used to lend credence to one hypothesis over others? Let's consider three such criteria that House employs to decide which hypothesis is preferable.

Simplicity

The criterion of simplicity has an episode named for it, "Occam's Razor." As Foreman summarizes Occam's principle,

"The simplest explanation is always the best." House, naturally, picks at this imprecise summary: holding that a stork is responsible for the appearance of a new baby is much simpler than citing the complex process of biological reproduction, but that does not mean the stork hypothesis is better. Nor does Occam's Razor say that it is. Occam's Razor literally says that entities (things) should not be multiplied unnecessarily. In other words, don't assume any more than you need to in order to explain the data. Thus, the Razor should be wielded only after the hypotheses in question have been shown to be of otherwise equal explanatory value. Positing that babies are deposited by storks is a lousy explanation, because it doesn't actually explain anything: Where do the storks get the babies? Why do the storks bring babies to some families and not others? Why doesn't anybody find feathers? Biological reproduction, on the other hand, is complex, but it accounts well for the observed data and leads to predictions that have been confirmed by testing.

So, Occam's Razor tells us that if you have two or more theories, all of which are consistent with the data at hand and are equally well supported with regard to making and confirming predictions, there is reason to prefer the simpler theory. This leads naturally to two questions: (1) what constitutes simplicity, and (2) why should we believe that, all things being equal, simpler is better? House poses the first question when, in response to Foreman and Cameron's claim that one disease is a simpler explanation than two independent diseases, he asks:

> Why is one simpler than two? It's lower, lonelier . . . is it simpler? Each one of these conditions is about a thousand to one shot. That means that any two of them happening at the same time is a million to one shot. Chase says that cardiac infection is a ten-million-to-one shot, which makes my idea ten times better than yours. ("Occam's Razor")

Here House is arguing, correctly, that simplicity isn't everything—one must also consider the probability of each event happening. But the first line addresses a more abstract and difficult issue: what makes one explanation simpler than another? Consider the previously mentioned situation in which House dreams about a patient (the marine) before meeting him. Hypothesis A says that House really dreamed of a generic marine and his mind superimposed the patient's face on the dream character retrospectively. Hypothesis B says that House saw the patient before, though he didn't consciously remember, and around the same time the patient was admitted something triggered this memory that surfaced in the form of a dream. Hypothesis C says that House is psychic. How should we rank these hypotheses in terms of simplicity? Intuitively, Hypothesis A seems simpler than B; both require assumptions about the nature of memory, but A does not depend on the confluence of so many events. What about C? It is certainly the simplest to state—three words. But it introduces a whole realm of possible experiences that we don't know much about and that run contrary to our ordinary understanding of how people know things. In this case, at least, it doesn't seem that simplicity is just a matter of the number of things or parts involved but may also include the kinds of assumptions that are made. Thus, although we can often identify clear cases where one explanation is simpler than another, actually offering a definition of simplicity is no simple matter.

This brings us to the second question: why should we believe that simpler is better? A simpler theory is easier to understand, but why assume that the truth will be easy to understand? Perhaps we can attack the issue from the opposite end. Cumbersome, opaque theories more easily hide their flaws and weaknesses, whereas the shortcomings of a simple theory are apparent. So, *not* finding any serious errors in a simple theory might be a better indicator of the truth of the theory than not finding any serious errors in a complex theory would be. In addition, complications are sometimes added to theories when their defenders are desperately trying to hold onto them in the face of counterevidence. A classic example of this phenomenon occurred in the debate over the structure of the solar system. An older theory, held by the philosopher Aristotle among others, maintained that the sun and the planets move in circular orbits around Earth. Unfortunately this model did not match well with observations of where the planets appeared in the night sky. So, the defenders of this theory added orbits upon orbits ("epicycles") to account for the discrepancies, resulting in an amazingly complex system. In contrast, a newer theory was able to do away with all these complications by simply positing that planets, including Earth, travel in elliptical orbits around the sun. Thus, in this case, complexity was a symptom of an ailing theory.

Elegance and Other Aesthetic Considerations

Toward the end of "Occam's Razor," when it seems that House's explanation for his patient's problems has been disproved, he laments:

House: It was so perfect. It was beautiful.

Wilson: Beauty often seduces us on the road to truth.

House: And triteness kicks us in the 'nads.

Wilson: So true.

House: This doesn't bother you?

Wilson: That you were wrong? I'll try to work through the pain.

House: I was not wrong. Everything I said was true. It fit. It was elegant.

Wilson: So . . . reality was wrong.

House: Reality is almost always wrong.

Here, and elsewhere, House shows an aesthetic appreciation for certain hypotheses, finding it viscerally painful when a beautiful explanation gets trampled by ugly facts. When he exclaims of a diagnosis, "It fits! It explains everything!" he is not merely stating that the hypothesis is consistent with the evidence; he is saying that it rocks! Consider the explanation House is referring to in the dialogue above. The patient has a laundry list of symptoms. No single disease can account for them all. But, House conjectures, suppose he started with just one symptom, a cough, which was treated erroneously with a particular medication that impairs cell regeneration. That would lead to all the observed symptoms, in exactly the order in which they appeared, owing to different rates of cell replacement in different organs. House has supplied a simple narrative that brings order to a chaotic mishmash of phenomena, a narrative that highlights general truths about human nature such as "We tend to overtreat simple ailments" and "Everyone screws up." He's right—it is beautiful, it is elegant.

Elegance includes, but goes beyond, mere simplicity. It is simplicity, plus power, plus beauty and style. Do such aesthetic considerations have any place in science, or are they, as Wilson suggests, a distraction from the road to truth? It's hard to say. Clearly many successful scientists are motivated by elegance. Nobel Prize–winning physicist Leon Lederman has stated, "My ambition is to live to see all of physics reduced to a formula so elegant and simple that it will fit easily on the front of a T-shirt."[3] Whether the inclination toward aesthetics in contemporary theoretical physics is positive or negative is currently a matter of debate.[4] But it is probably no coincidence that great triumphs in our understanding of the world, such as Kepler's laws of planetary motion and Einstein's theory of general relativity, have also been triumphs of elegance.

In connection with aesthetic considerations, let's briefly discuss one other feature of hypotheses that House tends to favor: novelty. As he puts it, "Weird works for me" ("Kids"). House offers a compelling reason to prefer weird symptoms: "Bizarre is good. Common has hundreds of explanations. Bizarre has hardly any" ("TB or Not TB"). That is, unusual symptoms are consistent with far fewer diagnoses than common symptoms are. If your patient turns orange, you'll get home sooner than if your patient complains of fatigue. But remember, these criteria are supposed to be considerations in favor of certain *explanations*, not in favor of certain *symptoms*. Still, House can make a reasonable case that, at least in his practice, novel explanations (diagnoses) have a higher chance of being right than do mundane explanations. As he chastises Foreman in the pilot episode, if a patient has some everyday illness, her family doctor will diagnose it and it will never even reach House's office. Given that House tends to see patients only after a gamut of other doctors have failed, it's likely that the diagnosis in question will be something weird. This presumption generally works well, though it had deadly results in "House Training," when it turned out that the patient's symptoms were caused by a simple staph infection.

As an offshoot of novelty, House also prefers diagnoses that are, well, funny: "So air is keeping him from breathing air. Let's go with that for irony" ("Spin"). Unless we assume that God exists and has a sense of humor, I can't see any plausible defense of the claim that amusing explanations are more likely to be true than dull ones. But it certainly does make for good television!

Origin

Finally, "origin" is a fancy way of saying that House prefers his own hypotheses to those of others. When trying to divert his team's attention from his legal difficulties with Lieutenant Tritter, he flippantly describes his approach:

> Cameron: What are you going to do?
>
> House: I thought I'd get your theories, mock them, then embrace my own. The usual.

The fact that he's right and somebody else is wrong is a big positive in House's book, and if he wins a bet in the process, all the better. Getting one's ego involved to the point that ownership of a particular explanation is taken to count in favor of the explanation could become a serious handicap; it could compromise one's objectivity. But I don't think House has fallen into this trap. Sure he wants to be right. So does everybody else. House would probably argue that he is just more up-front about this desire than are people who value humility. When Cuddy complains that he always assumes that he is right, he retorts, "I don't. I just find it hard to operate on the opposite assumption" ("Pilot"). So House operates full tilt on the assumption that he is right, until he gets evidence to the contrary. Since he clearly has no problem switching to a new theory when the old one fails to pan out, his preference for his own hypotheses isn't harmful.

Furthermore, there may actually be good reason to prefer a diagnosis simply because House made it. After all, he is "almost always eventually right" ("No Reason"). Although not a positive feature of the explanation itself, one could reason inductively from past successes to justify, when in doubt, favoring House's theories. As the *X-Files'* Fox Mulder presents this line of reasoning:

> Scully, in six years, how . . . how often have I been wrong? No, seriously. I mean, every time I bring you a new case we go through this perfunctory dance. You tell me I'm not being scientifically rigorous and that I'm off

my nut, and then in the end who turns out to be right like 98.9 percent of the time? I just think I've earned the benefit of the doubt here.[5]

The Great Puzzle

The universe, according to House, is a great puzzle. The answers are sometimes hidden from us, but they are always there. As he comments in "Half-Wit," "Just because it's inexplicted doesn't mean it's inexplicable." House holds fast to the idea that the reasons behind his patients' symptoms are indeed explicable, and he employs both standard scientific methods and more creative criteria to zero in on these reasons. By using factors such as simplicity, elegance, novelty, and origin to weigh one explanation against another, he raises interesting philosophical questions about the criteria themselves, such as "What constitutes simplicity?" and "Should aesthetic values, like elegance, count in favor of the truth of an explanation?" The answers to these questions are elusive pieces of the puzzle, but ones that House doesn't mind rooting around for a bit on the way to finding his diagnoses.

NOTES

1. G. W. Leibniz, *Principles of Nature and Grace, Based on Reason*, section 7, in *Philosophical Essays*, ed. and trans. Roger Ariew and Daniel Garber (Indianapolis: Hackett Publishing Company, 1989); see also *The Monadology*, section 32.

2. Peter van Inwagen, *Metaphysics* (Boulder, CO: Westview Press, 1993), 135.

3. Leon Lederman, *The God Particle: If the Universe Is the Answer, What Is the Question?* (New York: Dell Publishing, 1994), 21.

4. See Jim Holt, "Unstrung: In String Theory, Beauty Is Truth, Truth Beauty. Is That Really All We Need to Know?" *New Yorker*, Oct. 2, 2006.

5. Chris Carter, "Field Trip," *The X-Files*, 20th Century Fox/Ten Thirteen Productions (1999).

THE SOUND OF ONE HOUSE CLAPPING: THE UNMANNERLY DOCTOR AS ZEN RHETORICIAN

Jeffrey C. Ruff and Jeremy Barris

If you understand, things are just as they are; if you do not understand, things are just as they are.

—Zen proverb

House, Zen, and Making Sense

So an ancient once said, "Accept the anxieties and difficulties of this life." Don't expect your practice to be clear of obstacles. Without hindrances the mind that seeks enlightenment may be burnt out. So an ancient once said, "Attain deliverance in disturbances."

—Zen Master Kyong Ho (1849–1912)[1]

House's words and actions violate expectations. He speaks unprofessionally, rudely, and apparently irresponsibly. He violates confidences, ignores the wishes of his patients, holds back necessary information from both colleagues and patients, and breaks promises. Paradoxically, the results of these unethical practices are that patients and colleagues discover their true concerns and commitments, or find ways of fulfilling their commitments that weren't available to them before.

While the unmannerly doctor and the writers who give him such great lines may not have studied Eastern philosophy, House's rhetoric parallels certain forms of expression in Zen Buddhism. A koan, for example, is a Zen riddle or paradox like "What is the sound of one hand clapping?" It's not clear what an answer to this question would even look like, but pondering, reflecting, and meditating upon it can stretch the mind until its limits change, and so lead to insight. Like Zen rhetoric, House's rhetoric typically works by unsettling the assumptions of his audience (and, just as important, his own assumptions) about what does and does not make sense, with the result that new possibilities and solutions become available.

House constantly insists that "everybody lies." (In season three he goes so far as to say, "Even fetuses lie.") House is consistent in this attitude regardless of whether the lies are due to genuine dishonesty, lack of self-knowledge, embarrassment, or ignorance.

For example, in the episode "Sleeping Dogs Lie," Hannah planned to leave her girlfriend Max but didn't tell her, so that Max would give her part of her liver. Again, as we found out at the end of that episode, Max gave part of her liver with the hidden motive of preventing her partner from leaving her.

And in "Cursed," Jeffrey had spent time in an Indian ashram and contracted a tropical disease without realizing it, but he didn't mention that period of his life to his doctors because he was embarrassed about it. This suggests that what House might mean by "Everybody lies" is something like "People don't know how to speak in a way that is appropriate to the situation," or "Patients and doctors often make up their minds ahead of time when they don't actually know what's going on and as a result don't actually know what's important."

In these examples, House's starting point is that no one (not even he) knows or understands what is going on. Sometimes he may insist that he knows and is right, but at those times he also mocks people for trusting his diagnoses. Worse still, everyone involved may not even know *how to begin* to understand what is going on. Or everyone, including House, may be so stuck in their habitual—and therefore quite possibly arbitrary—ways of making sense that no one has any idea what the *genuine* sense is of any of the central things that are going on. As a result, they can't start a genuine exploration of the situation without unsettling all of their existing ways of making sense of it.

This state of not knowing how to begin to make sense, and of having to deal with that situation, reflects what the Zen tradition sees as a very basic and deep characteristic of life in general. We can't make sense of our lives as a whole. To do that, we'd have to be able to step outside of our lives and *see* them as a whole, and of course we can't do that. All our ways of making sense are parts *of* our lives, so that if we could step outside our lives, we'd of course also step outside all our ways of making sense! The result is that the idea of making sense of our lives as a whole literally doesn't make any sense.

But to make sense of our lives and the things that happen in them, we *need* to be able to get a grip on them, to make sense of them, as a whole. As a result, the Zen tradition advises us to go right ahead and step outside of sense itself, *altogether*. The standpoint that would allow us to get a perspective on our lives and sense as a whole is the standpoint, or starting point, of *not* making sense.

As we've been saying, the situations House deals with *already* don't make sense. But the problem is the same: if *nothing* central to the situation makes sense, then to have a real understanding of the situation we have to find a *wholly new* way of making sense. And to find a wholly new way of making sense we need to start with not making sense in the familiar ways. Only by not thinking and acting in sensible or "fitting" or appropriate ways can we *arrive at* sense and sensible action.[2]

Now we can see how House's rude, aggressive, or manipulative behavior in these circumstances is effective in dealing with the senselessness of the situation, or the kinds of lies, confusion, and lack of insight that obscure the genuine sense of the circumstances. His abrasive behavior eventually opens the possibility to everyone involved that "nothing is as it seems," and that "assumptions or presuppositions" won't do anyone any good in a world where nothing central to the situation makes its own genuine sense.

A Style of Behaving Ethically

To develop your . . . clear, unbiased judgment, it
is important to give up, or to be ready to give up
everything, including your understanding of the
teaching and your knowledge. . . . Then you will be
able to tell what is good and what is bad.

—Zen Master Shunryu Suzuki (1904–1971)[3]

In the episode "DNR" Foreman opts to do nothing for an ailing jazz musician because the trumpet player doesn't want any more treatments (he believes that he's dying of ALS). Throughout the episode Foreman maintains that House doesn't know the difference between right and wrong, because House treats the patient against his wishes. He further criticizes House in this (and other episodes) for not taking what everyone else knows are the right, socially proper, or legally safe actions.

In defense, House points out to Foreman that "if you do nothing, it doesn't matter which one of us is right." The jazz musician himself, when talking to Foreman about whether House or his own physician is right, tells Foreman, "You gotta pick one, son." In this kind of situation it's only by acting, *without* properly knowing what one's doing, that one can make *any* constructive difference to the situation at all. The alternative is to ensure that one will *never* find out the right thing to do, and so to commit oneself to being *completely* thoughtless and irresponsible about the true situation.

The dialogue from "DNR" suggests that "what is right" is not a matter of *understanding* what is right. In other words, we don't reach what is right by thinking or believing, by making sense. Instead, what is right is something that one *does* or performs. More than this, what is right is discovered only *through* that action and is recognized only as a result of it. So what one *thinks* is correct or incorrect matters less than getting the *actions* right. House is always active (or proactive) rather than being reactive. He doesn't allow law, expectation, assumption, social acceptability, or certainty to proscribe or prescribe his actions.

We shouldn't go overboard here: this doesn't mean that we should always act or always make choices without regard to sense. Rather, there are particular situations when, and particular ways in which, we need to act without properly knowing what we're doing.

House routinely deals with situations in which no one can see the (genuine) sense of anything central to the problem, including what the problem *is*. And so no one really *knows* what the "end" or goal might be. As a result the responsible, the right, thing to do is to *unsettle* the apparent sense of the whole situation so that we can *find out*, among many other things, what the "end" is.

In fact, the result of House's inappropriate interactions with his patients and colleagues is generally (not always, of course—House does make mistakes!) that the true needs of the participants' situations, as recognized by the participants themselves, are met in ways that turn out not to conflict at all with the means by which he got there. House's style achieves this in one, or both, of two ways. His tactics often bring out a wider range of considerations than were previously recognized, considerations important to the participants themselves, and the end result does justice to these, as well as the original, considerations. Or when the participants' true concerns or commitments in the situation turn out to be different from what they had first thought, the whole framework of ethical obligations that had protected those particular concerns becomes unimportant.

In "Mob Rules," for example, Bill, the "mob" brother of Joey, the equally "mob" patient, refuses to accept that Joey has hepatitis C, and still less to let him be treated for it, because he could only have contracted it through gay sex, and the accusation of being gay would harm his reputation in the "mob" irreparably and very dangerously. In fact, once Bill is forced to recognize that the truth of the situation is that Joey really *is* gay and actually wants out of his life in organized crime, then Bill's understanding of the illness and the circumstances change completely. At that point, the very real danger he had resisted turns out to be manageable in a completely unexpected way. And the true problem with Joey's safety, that Bill's ideas of how things make sense had stopped him from seeing properly, can be dealt with, too.

Again, in the episode "House vs. God," the patient's father supports his son throughout the episode against House's antireligious commitment to science, but he himself ultimately switches his allegiance to House once House discovers— through his disrespectful skepticism—that the boy had had a sexual affair and so betrayed his own religious principles. In the light of that discovery, all the previous religious conflicts became irrelevant. Everything relevant (or central) to the problem they were dealing with was the result of the boy's betraying his own religious principles. And so it turned out that it was perfectly fine, from *everyone's* point of view, for House to have suspended those same principles in that situation.

It's important to notice that House does not engage in a simple "end-justifies-the-means" approach to ethics. That kind of approach might suggest, for example, that mistreating or lying to a patient in certain circumstances could directly lead to the patient's recovery, and therefore the lie or mistreatment would be justified because it leads to a "good" result. Yet this is explicitly *not* the way that House justifies his actions. In fact, most often, he doesn't justify his actions *at all*.

House's emphases on action rather than thought and on proactive lack of justification, taken to the point of having no concern *with sense at all*, bear strong similarities to Zen techniques and rhetoric. In the classical Zen stories, masters seek to teach their students to be open to the world "just as it is," and to their own realizations. The master may do this by refusing to answer questions or by answering them nonsensically, by giving one answer in one circumstance and an entirely conflicting answer in similar circumstances, by striking the student, throwing a shoe at them, barking like a dog, or by any number of other counterintuitive and possibly rude responses. The Zen master does not impart data or discursive knowledge directly to students, because "insight" or "enlightenment" is not information that a person learns (like algebra or the metric system). Instead, it's based on a change in the way a person looks at and is oriented to the world, in its entirety.

House's abrasive behavior and the ethics it involves work in a similar way. House doesn't do what he does to produce a cure, but to find out what the problem is. If his actions do directly produce a cure, that's an accidental by-product—and for his purposes, as he complains at such times, an *unsatisfactory* one. As a result, he doesn't and can't know what the "end result" of his behaviors will be. He doesn't know why the patient is actually sick. He doesn't know what will happen when he tricks them, or bullies them, or tries dangerous medical procedures.

House acts in order to destabilize everyone's expectations (his own, the patients', his interns', the staff's, and so on). He shakes everything up not to get a particular result, but in order to let the illness (or issue) reveal itself as it is, on its own terms. House repeats this process until someone (usually him, but sometimes the other doctors) has an insight into the problem. So, House's approach is to destabilize the situation repeatedly until an original insight emerges.

Once we've found the genuine sense of the situation, our normal standards for what's ethical and appropriate operate again in this new context of understanding. This is why we can still see House as rude and unconventional, instead of just seeing him as fitting in with the new situation. Actually, House goes through the whole business of being House *just so that he can* make sense of the situation, *on the basis of what he thinks of as sense before unsettling the sense of anything.* In other words, he is, all along, following the guidance of our normal, everyday standards for sense and appropriateness. House's and Zen's dismissal of sense and appropriateness is for the sake of, and depends on, those usual, everyday standards of sense and appropriateness.

As a result, perhaps the oddest thing about House and Zen is that, as well as being so very odd, they *also* turn out not to be odd in any way at all. In that way, they're kind of the wizards of odd. As Zen Master Shunryu Suzuki says in this connection, "How do you like Zazen [Zen practice]? I think it may be better to ask, how do you like brown rice? Zazen is too big a topic. Brown rice is just right. Actually there is not much difference."[4]

So Zen and House's behavior turn out not to be odd at all. *This* is what the Zen tradition means by such terms as "beginner's mind" or "ordinary mind"—that is, a mind that just does what it does and then discovers the next moment openly and without prejudgments. Zen practice focuses on eating, sleeping, walking, sitting, and solving the problems of the day as they arise. Zen practitioners contend that by paying attention to the simple, everyday issues, one can consequently understand very important or difficult issues.

In summary, House's behavior is like a Zen practice. It's a style of *discovering* what the right way to act *is*. It does this, as it must, by being without presuppositions, without expectations, without knowledge of end. Nonsensically, but truly, it's a way of acting to discover how to act, not a style that "knows" what's right in advance.

House's irresponsible rhetoric, then, turns out to be a way of living ethically.

A Way of Establishing Intimacy

[The practice of Zen] means returning, completely,
to the pure, normal human condition. That condition
is not something reserved for great masters and
saints, there is nothing mysterious about it, it is
within everyone's reach. [The practice of Zen] means
becoming intimate with oneself, finding the exact
taste of inner unity.

—Zen Master Taisen Deshimaru (1914–1982)[5]

It's House's rhetoric—not House himself—that achieves results. House is just as subject to the effects of his rhetoric as anyone else. In the true Zen spirit, there's no active "subject" here controlling or manipulating passive "objects." Instead, there's a "happening" or a "way" that the "subjects" and "objects" are only separate from in a limited way. House isn't successful because he's some kind of master of medical mysteries, but instead because he's committed to the practice of a kind of Zen rhetoric that will lead to answers with or without his conscious control of the process. The activity of diagnosis links the doctor, the patient, the puzzling disease, the circumstances, and the sense they all potentially make into a single event or "happening." As a result, we could say that House is just one of the instruments being used by the activity of diagnosis. In other words, House is "inside" the rhetoric; he's being performed by it and through it.

By his brutality and apparent indifference to humane considerations, House makes himself vulnerable to others' judgments, stripping himself of any protection of conventional respectability. And, equally, he does the same thing to others. As a result, his ongoing bonds with his friends and coworkers have no ulterior motives to rest on. The people involved are left with being connected only for the sake of that connection, pure, naked, and genuine. When professional courtesy, social politeness, and simple decency are all stripped away, then what remains is simply and genuinely the rhetoric, the style or way of the process, of discovery working its way through the experiences of each of the participants (doctors, patients, everyone involved).

House doesn't control the circumstance like some puppet master. Instead, he in fact undermines the control that *anyone* in the situation might (think they) have. He gives up control and strips others of control in ways that foster intense and very personal interactions. In this way, his rhetoric establishes profound human connection, or intimacy.

A Path to Truth, and a Method of Healing

A master in the art of living draws no sharp distinction between his work and his play; his labor and his leisure; his mind and his body; his education and his recreation. He hardly knows which is which. He simply pursues his vision of excellence through whatever he is doing, and leaves others to determine whether he is working or playing. To himself, he always appears to be doing both.

—François René Auguste Chateaubriand (1768–1848)[6]

Because House's rhetoric unsettles expectations and so allows solutions to emerge that the old expectations prevented, House's rhetorical style is also a way to truth. In fact, it's not only a way of discovering truth, but also a way of *becoming* what one truly is, since, as we've seen, it allows people *themselves*, and their relations to each other and to what they value, to emerge in their own naked truth.

We can see this, oddly and interestingly, in how he regularly dismisses his interns' suggestions (while demanding more of these suggestions!), and in how he typically interrupts their flow of thought by going off on silly tangents. He not only doesn't listen properly, but he actively makes sure that he's not listening properly. In this fashion he gets his own expectations and customary ways of thinking out of the way, and so opens himself (and sometimes also the disrupted speakers themselves) to noticing implications of what people are saying that he doesn't expect, and, what's more, that they themselves haven't been able to notice.

As it happens, the same reasons that make House's rhetoric a way to truth also make it a method of healing. First, because it's a way of finding the truth of the situation, it's a way of making it possible to find healing solutions. And second, in allowing the people themselves to emerge more truly and fully, it's already a different and deeper form of healing, in itself.

What's more, as we've discussed, the activity of diagnosis (of looking for the truth of the situation) links all the participants into a single process or event. As the Zen tradition emphasizes, this link is really so close that all the participants are in fact just different sides of one and the same "entity." This is the famous "nondualism" of Buddhism. One thing this means here is that a change in one part of the process also changes the other parts. As a result, for a doctor, finding the truth—which is a change in the doctor's understanding—is *already* also a healing change in the medical problem and the patient. We've seen this already right here, in that finding the truth allows us to see the patient and his or her problems completely differently, so that we are not dealing with the same issues any more, and *this* is what allows the healing to get under way (as in the examples discussed earlier).

So, from the point of view of what House is doing, talking about discovering the truth, and talking about "research methodology," is *already* talking about methods of healing. These can't be separated, because they're one and the same thing! It's this particular point that all of House's colleagues and friends fail to understand. House's closest friend, Wilson, often criticizes House by saying that he only cares about solving the puzzle and that he doesn't care about anything else (not the patient, families, colleagues, etc.). House often neither accepts nor denies these charges; most often he simply says something glib in response. However, here, House is playing with his buddies a bit (though whether he himself is fully aware of this is unclear); he's leading them on with a bit of a wink and a nod to the audience. For House, there's simply no difference between solving the puzzle and serving the needs of everyone involved.

It's also important to see that if what I am, what I do, and what I know are all parts of the same thing in this way, then House is not just strategically and cleverly *choosing* to be inappropriate, silly, self-centeredly petty, rude, and so on, any more than he's acting on what he objectively can't help being. What he *is* and what he chooses to do are one and the same thing. So it's true that he's choosing to act, but that choice also comes from what he simply *is*. In other words, House *is* all of these faulty things—and they are the medium (or part of the "way") of his virtues!

Zen Master Suzuki makes this comment:

> The most important point is to establish yourself in a true sense, without establishing yourself on delusion. And yet we cannot live or practice without delusion. Delusion is

necessary, but delusion is not something on which you can establish yourself. It is like a stepladder. Without it you cannot climb up, but you don't stay on the stepladder. . . . We shouldn't be disappointed with a bad teacher or with a bad student. You know, if a bad student and a bad teacher strive for the truth, something real will be established. That is [Zen].[7]

House Sitting

You must meditate upon and consecrate yourself wholly to each day, as though a fire were raging in your hair.

—Zen proverb

House is deeply flawed, yet he is also depicted as uniquely free. His utter commitment to his Zen rhetoric frees him to have insights into nearly unsolvable problems. His life is not especially happy, warm, or free from pain: these are the goals to which many people would commit their lives. Paradoxically (if compared to what many people want or expect from life), House is often depicted at the end of each episode as peaceful and content when he has had the clear insight that solves that week's case. His personal or professional life might be full of unknowns or even in shambles. This troubles him little. At the end of "Human Error," the last episode of the third season, for example, we find the atheistic House sharing a cigar with a deeply religious patient's husband, both of whom everyone thought House was abusing throughout the episode. They are discussing how all of House's interns either quit or were fired.

The husband: It's hard to lose your people. You must be upset.

House: I must be.

The husband: But you're not.

House: No, I'm okay.

The husband: What are you going to do?

House: God only knows.

When the rhetoric and its performative and proactive style have been practiced with clarity and focus, he accepts all other aspects of circumstance with Zen-style equanimity.

So we might perhaps sum all of this up with the thought that from House's point of view, it's not what you know, it's who you do.

NOTES

1. Mu Soeng, *Thousand Peaks: Korean Zen—Traditions and Teachers* (Cumberland, RI: Primary Point Press, 1996), 173.

2. We've slipped in "action" here and added it to "sense," and we'll see a little later that this is actually a very important connection for House and Zen—and that there is a very important and illuminating reason why it had to be just slipped in, a bit slyly and without appropriate explanation or justification! This is a little hint that our essay is up to some House or Zen tricks itself, and later we'll see why. We'll also see why the authors are not in control of those tricks, but are just as much subject (or object) *to* them and guided or redirected *by* them as are you, the reader!

3. Shunryu Suzuki, *Not Always So: Practicing the True Spirit of Zen* (New York: HarperCollins, 2003), 117. All subsequent quotes from Suzuki come from this text.

4. Ibid., 40.

5. Taisen Deshimaru, *The Zen Way to the Martial Arts: A Japanese Master Reveals the Secrets of the Samurai* (New York: Compass, 1982), 5.

6. Source unknown.

7. Suzuki, 41.

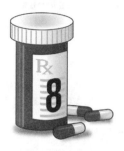

"BEING NICE IS OVERRATED": HOUSE AND SOCRATES ON THE NECESSITY OF CONFLICT

Melanie Frappier

"What's Wrong with Them?": Are House and Socrates Two Raving Lunatics?

House and Socrates. Two cases, same symptoms. House's best friends describe him as rude, arrogant, and offensive. He never misses a chance to sarcastically pick people apart. He refuses any administrative or clinic duty. His sharp mind has made him a leading expert in diagnostic medicine, yet he doesn't write up his medical cases for journals; the "ducklings"—Foreman, Cameron, and Chase—do it for him.

The only person who sometimes manages to control House is Cuddy, the dean of medicine and hospital administrator. While she admits that he is the best doctor she has,

House's obsession with his cases is at times a costly nightmare. He hides when on compulsory clinic duty. His unorthodox, and sometimes outright unauthorized, treatments lead to billing problems and lawsuits. His refusal to endorse a new drug costs the hospital a $100 million donation. He destroys the hospital's MRI machine, attempting to scan the bullet-riddled skull of a corpse (a scan Cuddy had, of course, forbidden).

House doesn't show any more concern for people than for financial matters. He bursts in on other doctors when they're with their patients, or calls them in the middle of the night to discuss *his* cases. Yet he doesn't listen to their opinions, turning down each of their answers with sarcasm and taking a vicious pleasure in humiliating them in front of their peers and patients. An "equal opportunity offender," House is aggressive and demeaning with his own patients.

Is House simply a "raving lunatic," or is his obnoxious behavior a symptom of a more serious condition? We could paraphrase House (in "The Socratic Method") and answer: "Pick your specialist, you pick your symptoms. I'm a jerk. It's my only symptom. I go see three doctors. The neurologist tells me it's my pituitary gland, the endocrinologist says it's an adrenal gland tumor, the intensivist . . . can't be bothered, sends me to a witty philosopher, who tells me I push others because I think I'm Socrates."

Socrates? If there was someone ancient Greeks thought was a pest, it was he. He was probably a stonemason by trade, but Socrates clearly preferred to spend his time discussing philosophy, nagging others with questions about truth, beauty, and justice. He didn't write anything himself, yet the oracle at Delphi declared, "No one is wiser." Bright young Athenians, like Plato and Xenophon, were Socrates' "ducklings" and immortalized him as the main character of their dialogues.

Because Socrates neglected his work in favor of philosophy, he was poor. Unable to properly provide for his children, Socrates was pursued throughout the city by his sharp-tongued wife, Xanthippe. While Xanthippe is remembered as the only person to have ever won an argument against Socrates—much like Cuddy is the only one who sometimes bends House's will—her admonitions had only a moderate influence on her strong-headed husband.

Like House, Socrates showed little empathy when engaging people in philosophical debates. While, unlike House, Socrates valued friendship, people were quick to point out that discussions with him were as "pleasant" as a stingray's electric discharge. Such unpleasantness was justified, however, because Socrates believed himself to be on a godly mission to show people that they didn't know anything. Part of this mission was to undo the work of the Sophists, who taught the art of winning arguments for the sake of winning arguments rather than achieving the truth.

Why stun and confuse people with ironical questions, if afterwards you only insult them and reject their answer? The answer lies in the so-called Socratic method.

"Nice Tries Are Worthless": First Know That You Don't Know

The Socratic method is based on the idea that knowledge is something that cannot be given. Rather, you have to discover it for yourself. So the only way to help someone else learn anything is by asking questions that will help that person reason his or her way to the truth. True Socratic professors do not lecture; instead they perform cross-examinations of their students to help them discover the weaknesses of their own positions. This Socratic method, House believes, is "the best way to teach anything apart from juggling chain saws."

There's a nice demonstration of a Socratic cross-examination in the episode "Three Stories." House, forced to play substitute teacher, asks medical students why a drug addict suffering from excruciating pain in a leg has tea-colored urine:

Student: Kidney stone.

House: Kidney stones would cause what?

Student: Blood in urine.

House: What color is your pee?

Student: Yellow.

House: What color is your blood?

Student: Red.

House: What colors did I use?

Student: Red, yellow, and brown.

House: And brown. What causes brown?

Student: Waste.

The student has gone from believing that the patient had two distinct problems—kidney stone and pain in the leg—to the belief that the unusually colored urine is not caused by kidney stones, but by a kidney's failure that may be related to the leg pain. Notice how House proceeds. Just like Socrates would, he asks his student to try to solve a very difficult problem: "Why is the urine tea-colored?" The first answer—"Because of kidney stones"—is only a *probable* answer, and both House and the student know this. So it's necessary to test the hypothesis further. First, House innocently asks questions that lead to answers seemingly supporting the student's initial conclusion, answers like "Kidney stones cause blood in urine," "Blood is red," "Urine is yellow." Then House, like Socrates would, goes on to secure a further statement that shows that the initial answer is wrong: if the problem was really a kidney stone, there would be no waste in the patient's urine.

Believing that our theory is the best possible one without looking closely at all the evidence is the worst blindfold we can have. The thing that most successfully guides us through changes in life is our ability to reason our way to new conclusions when faced with contradictions or ignorance. But to use reason properly, we must first realize that there is something that we don't quite get.

In Plato's dialogue the *Meno*, for example, Socrates asks a young boy a series of questions that make the boy realize that he doesn't know how to double the size of a square. Socrates is happy about this outcome and remarks: "At least it seems that we have made him more likely to find out the truth. For now he will be glad to search for it because he knows he does not know it, whereas formerly he might easily have supposed on many occasions that he was talking sense."[1] In "Three Stories," House reaffirms—more bluntly—the same idea. To the student who admits she doesn't know what causes the waste in the drug addict's urine, House cries: "You're useless. But at least you know it." To the male student trying to salvage a previous hypothesis, House simply throws a disdainful: "You know what's worse than useless? Useless and oblivious."

"Treat Everybody as If They Have Korsakoff's": The Role of Irony

While House and Socrates are often mean to their students, they usually do not insult them directly, preferring to throw in a few ironic remarks that say the opposite of what they really mean. In "Histories," for example, House throws a medical dictionary to two students perplexed over the inconsistent medical history of a patient, saying, "Oh! I'm just too nice. Here. It starts with C." There is a double irony at play here. First, we all know that House is not nice. Second, he is misleading the students about the illness, a kind of brain damage, known as Korsakoff's syndrome, which prevents patients from remembering new events and forces them to inconsistently fill their memory gaps with cues from their environment. Of course, Korsakoff's starts with a *K*, not a *C*.

House's irony is obviously meant to mock his students in a very funny way (at least for us). But for House, as for Socrates, irony has a more important role: to puzzle and perplex![2] The students are already confused and doubting themselves. Why is House playing such a mean trick on them? He's trying to give them a brainteaser that will start them thinking again and give them a clue to help solve their problem, *if* they interpret the puzzle correctly. By telling them he's too nice, it is clear to everyone—even those two students—that what House means is that he's a mean person. But why is he mean? That's the puzzle. The students innocently conclude that it's not nice to force them to look for the correct diagnosis themselves when it is obvious he knows it. They underestimate his meanness: giving them the dictionary is *not* meant as a suggestion on how to solve the problem. Just think about the sheer number of illnesses starting with *C*! The gesture itself is ironic: it is ridiculous for doctors to rely too heavily on authority, whether House or the dictionary. Observing the evidence at hand and thinking the case through is the only way to diagnose some-one. Had the students been more aware of how one learns and reasons, they would have picked up on this one.

Notice that the Socratic method does not transmit a lot of information in a small amount of time. That's not its goal. Rather, it aims to make students realize that they don't know as much as they thought they did. This *is* at odds with our current educational system, which tries to build students' self-confidence by emphasizing their accomplishments rather than their errors. So perhaps we're teaching students the wrong things. So-called facts are continuously disproved, and theories change. What students need is not to learn how the world is, but how to think *despite* the fact that we don't always know how the world is.

"Differential Diagnostics, People":
The Socratic Method of Hypothesis

Realizing that we don't know much is only the first part of the Socratic method. This is perhaps where House and Socrates differ the most. While Socrates was trying to make his fellow citizens realize how limited their understanding of the world was, House is more interested in solving medical mysteries that are already puzzling everyone. But here again House follows Socrates' advice, using the "second part" of the Socratic method, the "method of hypothesis."

Socrates' own "makeshift approach" is presented in Plato's *Phaedo* where Socrates explains to his student Cebes that we can't start our discovery of the world by observing everything about it. The sheer quantity of information we'd have to take into account if we tried to observe every aspect of a phenomenon would be such that it would "blind our soul" just like the observation of a solar eclipse would blind our eyes. At the beginning of "Three Stories," for example, House presents another leg pain case, that of a farmer. The students propose to take a family history of the patient, run a CBC, do a D-dimer, get an MRI, and perhaps perform a PET scan. When House tells them that the patient would've died if he'd been treated this way, a student cries out: "We had no time to run any tests; there was nothing we could do!"

So what *should* one do? In the *Phaedo*, Socrates tells Cebes: "In every case I first lay down the theory which I judge to be soundest."[3] Sounds like House's "differential diagnosis": first look at the different possible causes for the symptoms, then investigate the one that seems the most plausible. Sharp leg pain like the one the farmer has can be caused by exercise, varicose veins, injuries, and animal bites. As the farmer says he was in a field when he suddenly felt the pain in his leg where a puncture wound is now found, a snakebite seems the most likely solution. Adopting this avenue of research as a "working hypothesis" enables House to focus on the wound and discover—through an unsuccessful series of treatments for snakebites—that the wound was actually a *dog* bite.

"Make a Note: I Should Never Doubt Myself": Defending the Most Likely Solution

Given House's and Socrates' insistence on knowing we don't know, we might be tempted to conclude that the next step of the method of hypothesis is this: find further evidence in favor of our preferred diagnostic, while keeping in mind that we really don't know anything and being ready to abandon it as soon as new symptoms contradicting it appear. Yet in the *Phaedo*, Socrates tells Cebes that upon choosing a hypothesis, "whatever seems to agree with it—with regard either to causes or to anything else—I assume to be true, and whatever does not I assume not to be true."[4]

So next we should *assume we're right*? Coming from someone who claimed he knew nothing, this seems quite arrogant—even House-like! But actually, the arrogance both Socrates and House display is central to the Socratic method. When an exasperated Foreman reproaches House for his lack of humility after having repeatedly screwed up the diagnosis of trumpet player John Henry Giles, House snarls: "And humility is an important quality. Especially if you're wrong a lot." When Foreman cries out: "You've been wrong every step of the way!" House replies with a scowl: "Of course, when you're right, self-doubt doesn't help anybody, does it?"

House is telling Foreman that doubt will just prevent you from doing anything that would help you find the truth. You must accept the risk of being wrong, if you're ever to know you were right! If you're ready to discard your best hypothesis at the first sign of trouble, you'll never go anywhere with any of your opinions, because there'll always be some unexplained elements, some "yes, but . . ." options that will prevent you from pushing your hypotheses further. Before discarding your best hypothesis in favor of another, you need to give it the best, most convincing defense possible, in the same way that one should be given a strong defense by a good and convincing attorney before being convicted of a crime.

In other words, at the basis of House's and Socrates' stubbornness lies the belief that if you doubt your best judgment, you won't be able to make important decisions that will allow the case to progress. In the case of trumpet player John Giles, for example, House believes the musician could be suffering from Wegener's disease, a treatable illness. He therefore defies the patient's order not to resuscitate him ("DNR"). By contrast, Hamilton, Giles's treating physician, is convinced that the trumpet player is suffering from the incurable Lou Gehrig's disease and "pulls the plug." Had House not gone against the DNR order, Giles would have died. Had Hamilton not pulled the plug, House wouldn't have discovered that Giles did not have Wegener's and could breathe on his own. By both holding firm to their hypotheses, they made the case progress.

"Subordinates Can Disagree with Me All They Want, It's Healthy": The Necessity of Conflict

The Socratic method is thus a paradoxical one. On the one hand, to practice it you must admit that you do not know the truth. On the other hand, you must act as convincingly as if you were sure you knew the truth. But what if you're wrong? This is why once we have come up with a hypothesis, based on what we think we know, we *need* others to challenge us, to perform a cross-examination on *us*. We need them to question us to find out whether we've made any incorrect assumptions, used enough evidence to support our conclusion, or chosen our hypothesis based on unacceptable—yet perhaps unnoticed—personal prejudices. In the episode "The Socratic Method," House and his team have been investigating the deep vein thrombosis of a schizophrenic woman named Lucy. Despite the opinion of a legion of specialists, House wonders if the woman really is schizophrenic. When he calls his team to the hospital in the middle of the night to discuss his worries, Foreman complains:

> Foreman: If any of us did this, you'd fire us.
>
> House: Well, that's funny. I thought I encouraged you to question.
>
> Foreman: You're not questioning. You're hoping. You want it to be Wilson's. Boom. Give her a couple of drugs, she's okay.

House is aware he *could* be wrong. But how could he *himself* doubt any part of the solution *he* believes to be the correct one? He came to the conclusion that Lucy wasn't crazy based on what *he* thought was the most plausible argument. Others must seek out the argument's weaknesses for him. This is why it is so important for him to have Wilson oppose him and point out that Lucy's age and her decision to turn her son over to social services are not sufficient reasons to support his conclusion, because many schizophrenics develop symptoms late in life and are able to make some rational decisions despite their illness. While House is not convinced by Wilson's rebuttal, it is now clear to him that his own argument is rather weak. When he remarks to Wilson: "You think I'm crazy," the latter answers without any hesitation: "Well, yeah, but that's not the problem."

Here Wilson is wrong: his thinking that House is completely mistaken about Lucy *is* the heart of the problem. There is yet one unidentified presupposition that House and Wilson don't share in this case, and this is why they are arguing. In Lucy's case, their disagreement is about the symptoms that should be taken into consideration. Wilson believes that Lucy's liver tumor is unimportant and caused by alcohol consumption. House believes it is tied to her mental problems. As long as the problematic assumption is not explored (and they haven't discovered that Lucy can't metabolize copper properly), they only know that (at least) one of them is not looking at the situation objectively . . . but who? Until they find a common ground to resolve their disagreement, House and Wilson live in different realities.

"Reality Is Almost Always Wrong": Prejudices Hide the Truth

This idea, that people not sharing the same assumptions about the world are in a way not living in the same reality, is beautifully explored in "No Reason," the season two finale. House, having been shot, is taking care of a patient from the ICU room he's sharing with his aggressor. When House realizes he's hallucinating at least part of the time, he asks the imaginary version of his assailant how he can act in the real world if some of the information he has about the case isn't real. The attacker's answer is surprisingly simple: "You continue to throw out your ideas as you always would, but if they're based on faulty assumptions, your team will point that out."

In other words, we want our arguments to be objective, based on facts. But whether hallucinating or not, we always use unsupported assumptions—some correct and some incorrect—in our reasoning. How can we make sure we *do* have the facts? Oftentimes our background beliefs are so entrenched in our way of thinking that we don't even notice them. For example, when asked about the assumptions made in the case of the man with a swollen tongue in "No Reason," Foreman earnestly answers: "We do not have any. We're just guessing and testing." As the team quickly realizes, they are far from making innocent "guesses," for they were only looking at possible explanations that were in line with some highly probable—yet not certain—presuppositions: (1) medical tests are correct, if they give the same results three times in a row, (2) a biopsy provides a *representative* piece of the organ from which it has been harvested, (3) people who bleed where they are not supposed to have a bleeding problem, and (4) it is impossible to safely operate on a person with a bleeding problem.

Which of these claims correctly describes the world? Alone, House has no way of knowing: he could be dreaming, hallucinating, or just not seeing things as they truly are. His only hope is to "compare notes" with others, engage them about their beliefs, and see what there is in common. As the team soon discovers, not everyone shares the same assumptions. If Cameron is ready to question the tests, Chase trusts them. House seriously doubts that biopsies are necessarily representative. Now they can look at their disagreement and try to find out ways to resolve them. But had House been nice, had he said to every claim "I guess so" or "You're probably right," without asking his team to try to prove they were right, they would never have dug out the problematic assumptions, and they would never have found a way to test them.

In his delusion, House can keep acting as he always does, because he has not only used the Socratic method to help others get closer to the truth, but his obnoxious and arrogant behavior forces others to constantly question him. The fact is that whether hallucinating or not, House will defend his hypotheses with assumptions, some correct and some incorrect. To discover whether he is right, he has to uncover the problematic assumptions.

"You Can Disagree with Me. It Does Not Mean That You Have to Stop Thinking": Even Intellectual Conflict Is Difficult

But the role of objector that House and Socrates ask others to assume is an extremely difficult one to play. We're drilled into believing that our teachers, superiors, and leaders are right.

In a way, we're like Foreman, who, in the episode "The Jerk," goes against his best judgment and follows House's order to keep the patient on immunosuppresants after the latter tells him: "Look, you got two choices. Engage me in a futile argument and do what I asked or just do what I asked." And so most of the time we just stop thinking: we either accept others' positions—even if we disagree with them—or we're "tolerant" and let them "believe what they want." We almost always forget the third option (the one House hoped Foreman would choose): confront others on their beliefs.

Like Socrates and House, we need people to confront us. If others either agree with us or "agree to disagree with us" to avoid engaging us in debate, we'll stay confined to our own little reality. We need someone to stand up against us.

Yet very few people will do this for us, because they know we'll reciprocate and ask questions about *their* beliefs and opinions. Having one's most basic assumptions challenged is unpleasant, unsettling, and considered offensive in our society. Most people will simply refuse to do it unless . . . well, unless they are attacked and feel threatened. To learn anything, people like House and Socrates need others to question their opinions. Since others usually *avoid* conflict, they have no choice but to relentlessly attack people's beliefs from all sides, and harass them with questions and ironical remarks, until someone "awakes from their slumber" and strikes back, criticizing House's or Socrates' own assumptions.

Should we condemn such an attitude? If we think about it, an education that wouldn't challenge and change the ideas students already have would be a poor education indeed. And a doctor who wouldn't display a healthy skepticism about the current state of medicine wouldn't be more than a medical ATM, dispensing drugs according to some preestablished guidelines. Yes, just like physical fights, intellectual confrontations are painful. But they lead to our greatest discoveries.

At least with respect to knowledge, House is right: "Being nice *is* overrated."

NOTES

1. This translation of the *Meno* is found in Richard Robinson, *Plato's Earlier Dialectic*, 2nd ed. (Oxford: Clarendon Press, 1951). There are many different—yet all good—translations of Plato's *Meno*. Another good one is by W. K. C. Guthrie in *The Collected Dialogues of Plato*, edited by Edith Hamilton and Huntington Cairns (Princeton: Pantheon Books, 1961). To enable people to find the same passages in different editions, their lines are usually numbered. For example, this passage is numbered *Meno 84c*.

2. Gregory Vlastos pointed out this pedagogical use of irony in his article "Socratic Irony," which was published in his book *Socrates, Ironist and Moral Philosopher* (Ithaca, NY: Cornell Univ. Press, 1991), 21–44.

3. This passage is numbered *Phaedo 100a*. You can find it in *The Collected Dialogues of Plato*, ed. Hamilton and Cairns, 81.

4. Ibid.

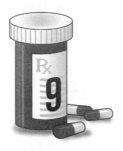

IS THERE A DAOIST IN THE HOUSE?

Peter Vernezze

In many ways, House is a figure at home in the Western philosophical tradition. As his diagnostic skills demonstrate, House places great emphasis on that cornerstone of Western philosophy, reason, and his rational-deductive powers are at the heart of the show's appeal. He also features another center-piece of Western thought: ego. Boy, does House have an ego! Introducing himself to one patient, he says, "I'll be the one saving your life today" ("Skin Deep"). About a successful diagnosis he declares, "Make a note. I should never doubt myself" ("Occam's Razor"). And when a CEO's staff determines he is the doctor in the region most able to treat her, he boasts: "Who da man? I da man" ("Control").

Reason and self (or ego) are two areas where Eastern philosophy differs from its Western counterpart. Recognizing the limits of human reason, the *Dao De Jing* informs us that sages "disseminate teachings that go beyond what can be said."[1] Highlighting the importance of humility, the *Dao De Jing* tells us that "the self promoting are not distinguished, show offs do not shine."[2] So connecting Gregory House with Daoism may seem like a nonstarter. But for all his apparent distance from the East, it is unlikely that House in fact can be fully understood without Eastern philosophy in general, and Daoism in particular.

Daoism (pronounced "dow-ism") was the great rival to Confucian thought in ancient China. Its legendary founder, Lao Tzu, was traditionally believed to be a sixth-century BCE contemporary of Confucius, although scholars now date the text ascribed to him, the *Dao De Jing*, to several hundred years after this time period. While Confucian thought was very much about playing one's appropriate role in society, Daoism stressed finding one's proper place in the universe and endorsed spontaneity rather than conventionality. Now that sounds a little more like House.

Read Less, Watch More Television

The dominant role that reason plays in the West is perhaps best illustrated by Aristotle's definition of man as a "rational animal." According to Aristotle (384–322 BCE), reason is the very essence of our being; it is what defines us as what we are. Stated at the beginning of Western philosophical tradition, this view never really leaves center stage. Some two thousand years later, René Descartes (1596–1650), the father of modern philosophy, wishing to discover what can be known with absolute certainty, concluded that while he may be dreaming or in some *Matrix*-like illusion, the existence of his mental-rational faculty alone is ultimately beyond doubt. He is, as he says, "a thing that thinks."

According to the Western philosophical tradition, reason gives access to the fundamental nature of reality. Plato (428–347 BCE) believed that the physical world we can see, taste, and touch was only semireal, too transient and passing to be taken seriously. Unchanging reality for Plato belongs to an eternal, unchanging world of Forms such as Beauty itself, known by means of unaided reason. Possessed of a similar faith in our rational abilities, the medieval philosopher and theologian Saint Thomas Aquinas (1225–1274) believed reason could prove the existence of God, as well as almost all important ethical and religious truths. To be sure, there have been reactions in the West against assigning this preeminent value to reason— Romanticism, for example. But from the start Western philosophy has pointed to reason as the dominant and defining human characteristic.

Befitting a character modeled after Sherlock Holmes, House puts his trust in reason. Indeed, the doctor calls the Socratic method, that famed style of rational inquiry named after the founder of Western philosophy, "the best way of teaching everything apart from juggling chain saws" ("The Socratic Method"). And Edward Vogler utters a widely shared belief when he declares to House: "My understanding was that you believed in rationality above all else" ("Role Model"). House's commitment to reason is not only theoretical but practical, as week after week we witness House's rational-deductive abilities: everything from using the symptoms of vitamin A overdose to unmask a faithless wife ("Paternity"), to determining that a humanitarian physician refusing treatment for TB in fact has a tiny but treatable pancreatic tumor ("TB or Not TB"), to (perhaps with a little luck) diagnosing hypothalamic dysregulation in a patient who has been nearly vegetative and wheelchair-bound for eight years and thus allowing him to return to normal life ("Meaning").

Such a character would seem to have little in common with the East's skepticism about reason's ability to attain knowledge of reality. Nowhere is this skepticism more apparent than in Daoism, as the first line of the Daoist classic *Dao De Jing* makes clear: "Way-making (dao) that can be put into words is not really way-making."[3] The notion of *dao* is at the heart of Chinese philosophy, occurring not only throughout the *Dao De Jing* but some eighty times in the *Analects* of Confucius. As Ames and Rosemont point out, "It is very probably the single most important term in the [Chinese] philosophical lexicon, and in significant measure, to understand what and how a thinker means when he uses *dao* is to understand that thinker's philosophy." Unfortunately, this is no easy task. We can say that the Chinese character for *dao* literally means "road" or "way" and add with Ames and Rosemont that "at its most fundamental level, *dao* seems to denote the active project of 'road building,' and by extension, to connote a road that has been made and hence can be traveled."[4] In a real sense, *dao* is to Eastern philosophy what "God" is to Christianity: the fundamental reality underlying all existence, except that we should not view the *dao* as a person or thing separate from the world but as ineluctably bound up with this world. To say, then, that this fundamental reality cannot be conveyed with words is to say that it is unknowable, beyond the grasp of reason.

It would seem to be a "slam dunk" case that House allies himself with the Western view emphasizing the power of reason, and not the Eastern view, which stresses reason's limitations. But House's attitude toward reason is much more complicated than might appear, as is realized when his fascination with a mentally ill patient leads Foreman to remark in surprise, "I thought he liked rationality" ("The Socratic Method"). No, it is declared, he likes puzzles. And other things, we might add, including medical soap operas, video games, and monster trucks.

When we might expect him to consult a medical journal or review case notes, House pops into a coma patient's room to watch a medical soap opera. While this sort of activity is hard to square with a reliance on rationality, it is completely in accord with the Eastern attitude that recognizes reason's limitations. As the *Dao De Jing* says, "Knowing when to stop is how to avoid danger."[5] House's seemingly perplexing behavior is actually an attempt to bring reason to a grinding halt. This is advice he not only follows himself but dispenses to others, as when he tells Cameron to read less and watch more television ("Control")! Far from being facetious, this comment is an attempt to convey in concrete terms a recognition of the limitations of reason. Like any good Daoist, House knows when to put on the brakes.

The Sage as Standard

Western philosophy commonly uses reason to determine the standard according to which the good person should act. Perhaps the best-known version of this approach to ethics is the categorical imperative of the great German philosopher Immanuel Kant (1724–1804): "Always act on that maxim that you can at the same time will to be a universal law of nature." The idea here is that correct moral actions are precisely those that are done according to standards that everyone in the same situation can follow.

This principle was driven home to me one day at an early age when while walking the family dog at a nearby park, I decided to ignore the evidence of his heeding nature's call. Suddenly, a man came running out from a house across the street and demanded I go back and clean up the mess. "What if everyone just let their dog do this in the park?" he demanded. Possessed of a philosophical spirit even then, I decided to chew over his proposition and soon saw his point. I enjoyed the park and certainly would not want my beloved baseball diamond covered in canine number two. So I did as he requested. Little did I then realize that I was being persuaded by a crude version of Kant's categorical imperative.

There is actually a little more to Kant's imperative than the dog poop example might lead one to believe. In order to see what more exactly there is, let's take one of Kant's own examples. Imagine, says Kant, that someone is thinking of taking out a loan but has no intention of paying it back. Now suppose that this person asked himself, what if everyone acted based on his standard of making a promise that one has no intention of keeping? Under such conditions, the person would have to admit that if everyone acted on the principle, it would not even be logically possible for him to consider his action because no one would take his—or anyone's—promise seriously. An action's contradicting itself if it were universalized—the fact that everyone's acting on the principle would make the action essentially impossible to consider in the first place—and not just the fact of its widespread adoption causing unpleasantness—was for Kant the telltale sign of its immorality.

Consider for a moment the relevance of this principle for House. Transplant lists exist in order to make painful but necessary life-and-death decisions about who will be eligible for the limited supply of organs. If those decisions are to be moral, Kant insists (and most would agree) that they need to be carried out in accordance with principles that are universalizable, that is, standards that apply to all those eligible for transplants. And generally speaking, this is what happens. The principles routinely invoked to decide who will get what organs—rules such as "People who have a better chance of survival should be given preference over those who have a worse chance of survival," and "Those with more life-threatening conditions should, all things being equal, be placed ahead of those whose conditions are less serious"—seem to pass Kant's universalizability test. That is, they can be applied equally to everyone. Such a system is "moral" and "just."

By contrast, it is precisely when an exception is made—when someone who is wealthy gets an organ even though that person is less healthy than someone who is of a modest income—that we view the system as unfair. Indeed, if doctors could put whomever they wanted on the list, regardless of whether the patient met the criteria necessary for inclusion, the list would cease to function in any meaningful way, as there would be no guarantee that anyone on the list was worthy of a transplant. But more important from Kant's point of view, it would cease to be moral. A doctor who contemplated circumventing the criteria for putting people on the organ transplant list would be in the same situation as the loan seeker contemplating making a promise he has no intention of keeping. In both cases, the universalization of the activity is inconsistent with the continued existence of the relevant practice. That is, just as no one would believe any promise made if lying were universalized, no one would think anyone on the transplant list was worthy of an organ because anyone could be put on the list.

But of course, this is precisely what House seems to do: violate the criteria in order to put who he wants on the list. When he discovers that a young female CEO in need of a heart transplant is bulimic, he baldly lies to the transplant committee, denying that there are any psychological factors that would disqualify his patient ("Control"). In a similar case, he artificially and against accepted practice shrinks the liver tumor of a schizophrenic patient when he learns that its current size makes it too big for a necessary operation ("The Socratic Method"). "Put whomever you want on a transplant list regardless of whether that person meets the accepted criteria" could simply not be universalized. If every doctor acted according to the standards of Gregory House, the basic concept of the transplant list would be undermined. In short, House's ethical standards, which include instructing his staff to "lie, cheat, and steal" ("Sex Kills"), are incompatible with the moral practice of medicine in our Western tradition that relies so heavily on rules and reason. This is why even Wilson says that House "should probably reread the ethical guidelines" ("Babies and Bathwater").

Of course, the fact that House is not acting on the categorical imperative does not by itself make him a Daoist. But it is pretty clear that House does not ascribe to the other great ethical system of the West, utilitarianism. A couple of things count against understanding House as utilitarian. To begin, a utilitarian would have to make a conscious effort to act in a way that would assure the greatest happiness for the greatest number of people. But there is no evidence that House gives any thought to bringing about the greatest happiness for the greatest number, nor do we have reason to believe that any of his actions have this as their intended result. Indeed, House is dismissive of the very idea of any such altruistic motivation. About a doctor who seems to be acting in a very utilitarian manner by curing TB in Africa, House asserts, "The great humanitarian is as selfish as the rest of us" ("TB or Not TB"). So it seems unlikely House is a utilitarian.

It's time to leave the West behind. There are some striking similarities between House's decision-making process and Daoist ethics. The *Dao De Jing* tells us that "sages are not partial to institutionalized morality."[6] Neither, we have seen, is House, who not only instructs his staff to "lie, cheat and steal," but is certainly not above carrying out such practices himself. More important, some of House's more troubling statements regarding his attitude toward patients find parallels in the *Dao De Jing*. When asked how he can treat someone he hasn't seen, he replies: "It's easy if you don't give a crap about them" ("Occam's Razor"). He tells an older patient who wants to take his wife off of life support that "you take your wife off life support and I'll have forgotten about it in two weeks" ("Sex Kills").

This level of unconcern for his patients doubtless strikes many viewers as one of House's more unattractive characteristics. But it is an attitude remarkably similar to the one we find in the *Dao De Jing*, where we read that "sages . . . treat the common people as straw dogs."[7] Straw dogs were sacrificial objects "treated with great reverence during the sacrifice itself, and then after the ceremony, discarded to be trodden underfoot."[8] Similarly, although House will sometimes risk his career for his patients, he obviously does so without any personal concern for the patient, who, it seems, he will soon forget about anyhow.

How to defend such an attitude? The Daoist sage substitutes his judgment for the moral status quo not merely because it is his but because it is in accord with the way of Heaven, the Dao. In such a moral universe, the wise individual becomes the standard of good and bad, right and wrong. Such an idea is difficult for many in the West to accept, and not without reason. But the idea of the "sage as standard" has a long history in Eastern thought. And what about House? We know that House has no difficulty viewing himself as a superior individual in his field, an expert whose judgment should be trusted. Such an enlightened individual does not necessarily concern himself with institutional morality; nor does he take particular care of the effects of his actions on the individuals they impact, because he knows those actions are in accord with a higher law. Of course, this is a pretty high opinion to have of oneself. But for someone who perceives himself as his profession's equivalent of Mick Jagger ("Sports Medicine"), Daoist sage is not much of a stretch—and might even be a bit of a letdown.

The Dao of Diagnostic Medicine

What should be our goal in life? From Aristotle onward, Western philosophy has provided one dominant answer. "All men," said Aristotle, "agree that this is happiness."[9] While there is nothing resembling a consensus concerning what exactly happiness is, one powerful and popular answer comes from the nineteenth-century utilitarian philosophers Jeremy Bentham and John Stuart Mill. According to this school of thought, a happy life is one that maximizes pleasure and minimizes pain. This seems to be the standard invoked when colleagues, coworkers, friends, patients, and even complete strangers refer to House as "miserable." Indeed, no single word, not even "arrogant," is used more frequently to describe him. House is no doubt dubbed "miserable" in large part because he is in a great deal of physical pain—the result of the botched operation on his leg. But others perceive House to be in psychological agony as well: isolated, irritable, obsessive, and, in his own words, "without a personal life" ("Cursed"). Indeed, Foreman's resignation at the end of season three comes precisely because House fails to live up to utilitarian standards of well-being—the fact that he is only momentarily "happy" when he has solved a case and for most of the rest of the time reverts to his miserable self.

But although there is a consensus that House is a failure according to a commonly invoked criterion of what makes a life worth living, we need to consider the minority opinion as well. This is stated most eloquently by a famous jazz musician under House's care, who recognizes in his doctor a passion he is all too familiar with:

> I got one thing, same as you. That obsessive nature. The reason normal people got jobs, wives, kids and hobbies is because they ain't got that one thing that hits them hard and true. I got music, you got this. ("DNR")

House's existence is here judged to be qualitatively above that of most people. While utilitarian and other commonly invoked standards of happiness will have a hard time justifying this claim, it is perfectly comprehensible to Daoism. In fact, Daoism speaks very little about happiness or related concepts. Instead, the goal of life is said to consist in achieving the Dao. Volumes have been written about what exactly this means. Let's settle for just one helpful illustration that is often used to describe the Dao in practice: that of an expert craftsman practicing his craft.

In the Daoist classic the *Chuang Tzu* we are told of a butcher, Cook Ting. A good butcher changes knives every year, but Ting is so gifted in cutting up animals that his knife is nearly twenty years old and is as sharp as if it were new. Cook Ting is a rather unorthodox practitioner, "cutting with his mind and not his eyes and following his spirit rather than his senses."[10] Nevertheless it works for him, and as a result of his expertise he is commonly recognized as a lover of the Dao. Since all professions have a Dao, we might well expect there to be a Dao of diagnostic medicine. Taking Cook Ting as our model, we can suppose the Dao of diagnostic medicine would combine a subjective passion with objective expertise and unorthodox methodology.

Is House, then, really a Daoist? No, there are many elements of Daoism that don't fit House. For that matter, I doubt that any system or theory can contain House. That's part of his appeal. But perhaps by looking beyond the West, we may come to a more complete and balanced view of an admittedly imbalanced but inherently intriguing individual.[11]

NOTES

1. *Dao De Jing*, translated and with a commentary by Roger T. Ames and David L. Hall (New York: Random House, 2003), 80. Although older translations used the transliteration *tao*, more recent translations use the more linguistically correct *dao*. In this chapter, I have chosen to use the latter.

2. Ibid., 114.

3. Ibid., 77.

4. *The Analects of Confucius*, translated, with an introduction by Roger T. Ames and Henry Rosemont (New York: Random House, 1998), 45.

5. *Dao De Jing*, 77.

6. Ibid., 84.

7. Ibid.

8. Ibid., 206.

9. Aristotle, *Nichomachean Ethics*, I.4, author translation.

10. *The Book of Chuang Tzu*, trans. Martin Palmer (New York: Penguin, 2006), 22.

11. This essay was written while I was serving as a Peace Corps volunteer at Sichuan Normal University in Chengdu, China. Many people there helped refine my thinking about Daoism and aided in the inspiration for this essay. I would like to especially thank Spencer Brainard and Sophie Tong.

PART THREE

"IT IS THE NATURE OF MEDICINE THAT YOU ARE GOING TO SCREW UP": HOUSE AND ETHICAL PRINCIPLES

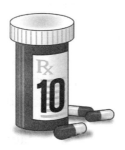

"YOU CARE FOR EVERYBODY": CAMERON'S ETHICS OF CARE

Renee Kyle

Rebecca: Is he a good man?

Wilson: He's a good doctor.

Rebecca: Can you be one without the other? Don't you have to care about people?

Wilson: Caring is a good motivator. He's found something else.

— "Pilot"

House doesn't like patients. In fact, he doesn't like people. He's cynical, insensitive, judgmental, and pessimistic. At times he acts inhumanely. But if there is a medical mystery to be solved, House is our guy. Still, if we were on the doorstep of death, would we *really* want House to be our physician? Does he represent what we want in a doctor?

The answer to this question, essentially, is no, and Dr. Allison Cameron shows us why. Where House doesn't give a crap about patients, Cameron demonstrates that she cares about every patient. There is, in fact, something gendered in the way that Cameron practices medicine and deliberates about moral problems that arise in her work. As we shall see, this is the domain of feminist ethics.

Beyond "Doctor Knows Best": Feminist Ethics

Ethics is the branch of philosophy that explores and analyzes moral problems. Ethics is concerned with questions such as: What kinds of moral principles and values should guide our actions? And what do we mean by right and wrong? Feminist approaches to ethics view such moral problems through the lens of gender. For example, a traditional approach to considering the ethics of surrogacy may have as its focus whether or not such an arrangement constitutes "selling" a child. A feminist analysis of the ethics of surrogacy would be incomplete without adequate consideration of the effects of these arrangements on the lives of the women involved.

All feminist approaches to ethics aim to interrogate and end systems, structures, and practices that oppress women. Feminists concerned with bioethics draw our attention to how health care policies, practices, and institutions can contribute to the oppression of women. Areas of particular concern include genetic screening, abortion, and the doctor-patient relationship.

The relationship between doctor and patient—its nature, its underlying values, what we think it ought to be—provides us with a good starting point for examining how House and Cameron practice medicine. Traditionally, the doctor-patient relationship grants authority based on scientific (medical) knowledge, and rejects subjective, experiential knowledge.

Because the majority of physicians are male, and the majority of patients are female, this relationship amplifies gender power differentials by privileging "masculine" knowledge over "feminine" knowledge.[1] If we know anything about House, it's that he very rarely listens to his patients' thoughts about their own illness. In "Que Sera Sera," a man suffering from obesity offers his opinion on the cause of his mystery illness. House arrogantly rejects the patient's opinion, asking: "Grocery stores giving away medical degrees with the free turkeys now?" In the "Pilot," House reinforces his authority over his patient, Rebecca, after she refuses any further tests or interventions for her mystery illness. House sees her refusal as tantamount to rejecting his own expertise:

House: I'm Dr. House.

Rebecca: It's good to meet you.

House: You're being an idiot. You have a tapeworm in your brain, it's not pleasant, but if we don't do anything you'll be dead by the weekend.

Rebecca: Have you actually seen the worm?

House: When you're all better I'll show you my diplomas.

Rebecca: You were sure I had vasculitis, too. Now I can't walk and I'm wearing a diaper. What's this treatment going to do for me?

In "Family," House berates Wilson into believing that doctors do indeed know best, and consequently, they should persuade patients to make the "right" decision:

House: All you had to do was say, "Yes, I do." God knows that's a phrase you've used often enough in your life.

Wilson: It was a mistake every time. Give it a break. They said yes.

House: That's not enough for you. You need them to feel good about saying yes.

Wilson: I treat patients for months, maybe years, not weeks like you.

House: I'm taller.

Wilson: If they don't trust me, I can't do my job.

House: The only value of that trust is you can manipulate them.

Wilson: You should write greeting cards.

House: Giving parents the chance to make a bad choice was a bad choice.

Wilson: At least it would've been their choice.

House: One they'd regret at their son's funeral.

House's "doctor knows best" approach to health care seems especially unethical because he refuses to form relationships with his patients. Instead, House relies on his team to establish relationships with his patients, sending his ducklings to gather medical and personal histories, explain procedures, and gain consent. Free of the responsibilities that accompany caring about patients, House can get on with the job of putting together the pieces of the medical puzzle. When he does finally interact with his patients, it's rarely a warm and fuzzy doctor-patient chat.

House is in constant conflict with Cameron, the duckling who cares so much. Cameron believes her relationship with the patient is integral to providing good health care because it is within this relationship that the honest exchange of information occurs. It is no coincidence that the battles between House and Cameron over patient care are fought along the lines of gender. The ethic of care, placing relationships at the center of moral decision making and action, guides Cameron's professional practice and is a form of ethical deliberation most commonly associated with women.

"It Almost Looks Like He's . . . Caring": The Ethic of Care

Carol Gilligan pioneered the ethic of care with her book *In a Different Voice*, which offers an account of women's moral development as an alternative form of moral reasoning.[2] Gilligan and other care-focused feminists argue that ethical theory tends to reflect only the traditional approach to moral deliberation known as the ethic of justice, which encourages the application of abstract, universal rules and principles to moral problems, appealing to notions of impartiality, independence, and fairness. For example, consider the scenario in which a person is thinking about stealing a loaf of bread, which he cannot afford to buy, in order to feed his family. A person who ascribes to the ethic of justice is likely to conclude that although feeding a family is important, the man should not steal the loaf of bread because stealing itself is morally wrong. It is worth noting that House does not exemplify the ethic of justice; indeed, his manipulation and deception of Cuddy and Wilson to support his own Vicodin addiction show that House is rarely interested in doing what is morally right. After interviewing women about the kinds of values that guide their decision making, Gilligan found that the ethic of justice was more likely to be adopted by men than women and argued that this type of reasoning was geared toward masculine language and experience. In an effort to better include the voices of women in moral theory, Gilligan developed an understanding of the ethic of care. In this ethic, the primary consideration in making moral decisions is to maintain and nurture attachments to others. The ethic of care recognizes our responsibilities to others and acknowledges the moral relevance of emotions that accompany caring for another. It also values the claims and experiences of those we care for, and recognizes that self-hood is constructed through, and by, one's relationships with others.[3]

Cameron is a powerful example of how the ethic of care can inform professional practice in a health care setting. She works hard to build trust in her relationships with her patients, consistently advocating on their behalf, and refusing to deceive, lie, or bully in order to acquire information, even when she is ordered to do so. As House notes, when presented with a problem, Cameron always attempts to find an answer that involves minimal harm to the parties involved: "Figures you'd try and come up with a solution where no one gets hurt" ("Heavy").

Cameron values her relationships with her patients, yet her ability to genuinely care for them amuses, bewilders, and annoys House. Cameron's practice is guided by her sense of responsibility to her patients, in spite of their perceived flaws, difficult personalities, and morally questionable behavior. In "Informed Consent," House reveals to Cameron that their patient, Ezra, a world-renowned physician, conducted ethically questionable research during his career. House uses this information in the hopes of getting Cameron to abdicate her responsibilities to the patient:

Cameron: So you're okay with what he did.

House: Doesn't matter what I think. It's what you think that's relevant.

Cameron: Because, if I think less of him, I'll help you more? You're wrong. The fact that a patient did bad things doesn't change anything. He still deserves to have some control over his own body.

Cameron's practice is also guided by identifying, and attending to, the particular needs of others as they occur in the context of their doctor-patient relationship. This skill seems to be something that House envies, but is unable (or unwilling?) to develop. In "Maternity," the team races against the clock to identify an unknown epidemic affecting newborns. To prevent the spread of infection, the parents are forbidden to have skin-on-skin contact with their children. While carefully changing the linen on one of the baby's cribs wearing protective clothing and gloves, Cameron notices the baby's parents looking at this procedure from outside the room. We see her immediately empathize with the parents as she remarks to Chase: "Imagine not being able to touch your own baby." To enable the parents to have some contact with their sick daughter, Cameron invites them to hold their daughter while the medical staff changes the bed linen. House assumes Cameron's empathy is rooted in similar experience rather than in her ability to appreciate the suffering of others:

> House: Chase told me about that idea you had, the parents holding the baby. Where'd you get that? Did you lose someone? Did you lose a baby?
>
> Cameron: You can be a real bastard.

And again in "Que Sera Sera":

> House: All right, I give up, who was it? Who in your family had the weight problem?
>
> Cameron: You think I can only care about a patient if I know someone else who's been through the same thing?

House doesn't believe the relationship between doctor and patient entails the responsibility to care. When, on rare occasion, House does genuinely care for one of his patients it's largely because he sees aspects of himself in the patient, or recognizes that they share an experience or history. For example, in "Half-Wit," House's patient Patrick is a man who, as a result of a brain injury in childhood, plays the piano masterfully. House's connection with Patrick is fostered by his own love of playing the piano. Similarly, House's own experience of becoming suddenly impaired creates a connection with Stacy's partner Mark, who becomes temporarily disabled and seeks House's advice ("Need to Know"). In the absence of parallels between patients' circumstances and his own life, House just doesn't seem to care for his patients at all.

Where House tends to view each patient as an abstract individual, Cameron sees her patients as embedded in a complex network of familial and social relationships. In making moral decisions, the ethic of care states that we have an ethical obligation to attend to the claims of those we care for, while avoiding hurting them. Cameron's commitment to this ethic is so strong that she becomes incensed when a patient, Hannah, makes a health care decision that seems to completely disregard the patient's caring obligations to her partner Max ("Sleeping Dogs Lie"). Confronting Hannah about her decision, Cameron implies that Hannah is selfish because her responsibilities to Max were not morally salient in her decision:

> Cameron: Aren't you at all concerned about what Max is going through right now? Shoving a tube up her rectum. Then they're going to swab her stomach just like I'm doing. It's going to hurt just like this hurts, which is nothing at all like the risk she's taking on the table. You don't love her, do you?
>
> Hannah: I'm not leaving her because I don't —
>
> Cameron: I'm not talking about the leaving, I'm talking about this. If you care for her at all, you won't let her do this blind.

Hannah: You'd really tell?

Cameron: Yeah.

Hannah: You'd die?

Hannah's question—would Cameron sacrifice her own life to ensure that she met her caring responsibilities?—points to an important philosophical criticism of the ethics of care.

Does Cameron Care Too Much?

The ethics of care is appreciated by most feminists as an important contribution to ethical theory because it both recognizes and validates women's experiences in an area of philosophy that has, for the most part, excluded women. That said, the ethics of care is not without its critics. Many feminists are concerned, and rightly so, that valorizing a moral theory based on a stereotypically female trait—caring—above other types of moral reasoning can lead women to think they should care about others at all times in all contexts, even if this caring incurs a personal cost.[4]

Cameron's behavior in certain situations provides a good example of how a commitment to an ethics of care may not always be appropriate in informing the way we approach moral problems, and indeed can interfere with our ability to perform tasks required of us. Consider Cameron's behavior in "Maternity." House orders Cameron to inform the parents of a sick newborn that their baby is extremely ill and is unlikely to survive the next twenty-four hours. Cameron doesn't convey the seriousness of the situation to the parents, and Wilson chastises Cameron for not telling them the truth:

Wilson: Allison, their baby's dying. If the parents weren't in tears when you left, you didn't tell them the truth.

Cameron: That's not how I see it.

Wilson: Do you want them blindsided? Want them coming up and saying, "My God, my baby died, why didn't you warn me?"

Cameron: So now it's about worrying about them yelling at us?

Wilson: No, it's about getting them prepared for the likely death of their child.

Cameron: If their son dies tomorrow, do you think they'll give a damn what I said to them today? It's not going to matter; they're not going to care; it's not going to be the same ever again. Just give those poor women a few hours of hope.

We learn later on in the season that Cameron watched her own husband die of cancer, and we can see how this experience guides her practice with patients who are facing a loss. What is unique about the ethic of care is that it promotes ethical deliberation that values the role of emotions—sympathy, empathy, sensitivity—in deciding what the best course of action would be.[5] What is problematic about Cameron's interactions with these patients is not that she uses her own experience to frame her actions; it is that she lets her emotions derail her professional judgment. In "Acceptance" Cameron is asked to inform a patient, Cindy, that she has terminal cancer. Witnessing Cameron and Cindy laughing in Cindy's hospital room, Wilson suspects that Cameron has not informed Cindy of the diagnosis:

Wilson: So I take it you were in there informing her?

Cameron: Well, I . . . I hadn't exactly gotten around to that, but I was just—

Wilson: Doing what? Making friends?

Cameron: Cindy's divorced. She doesn't have any kids, no siblings, both her parents are gone—

Wilson: It's not your job to be her friend. Do you understand?

It's here that Cameron reveals to Wilson that if she hadn't married her husband he would have died alone—much like Cindy. In this circumstance, Cameron moves beyond simply contextualizing the moral problem—she is reliving her own experience, unable to disentangle her own emotions from the problem at hand. Her own personal history interferes with, rather than contributes to, her professional practice. Of course Cameron shouldn't just reject the role of emotions in deciding what is morally best for her to do. Indeed, emotions can help us identify the needs of others and they can encourage us to view moral problems from a range of perspectives. Still, Cameron's overzealous caring often comes at a price, and it can compromise her professional practice. As the show progresses, this overzealousness increasingly seems to be driving her to adopt House-like tactics in the name of providing "care" to patients. In "Que Sera Sera," Cameron secretly (and unlawfully) administers an injection to a patient to prevent him from leaving the hospital against medical advice—"I didn't think he should be discharged so I gave him three grams of phenytoin. I wasn't going to just let him leave." Unfortunately, the price of caring too much for her patients means becoming more like House.

You're Basically "a Stuffed Animal Made by Grandma"

It is probably safe to say that there is no single approach to moral reasoning that delivers the best outcomes for all parties involved at all times. Yet, as the moral center of the show,

Cameron casts a spotlight on the ethic of care, providing a welcome contrast to House. Let's hope that underneath all that cynicism and complaining that Cameron is a "stuffed animal made by Grandma," House is taking notes.

NOTES

1. Susan Sherwin, "The Relationship of Feminism and Bioethics," in *Feminism and Bioethics: Beyond Reproduction*, ed. Susan M. Wolf (New York: Oxford Univ. Press, 1996), 57.

2. Carol Gilligan, *In a Different Voice: Psychological Theory and Women's Development* (Cambridge: Harvard Univ. Press, 1982).

3. Virginia Held, *The Ethics of Care: Personal, Political and Global* (New York: Oxford Univ. Press, 2006), 10–15.

4. Sandra Lee Bartky, *Femininity and Domination: Studies in the Phenomenology of Oppression* (New York: Routledge, 1990), 118.

5. Held, *Ethics of Care*, 10.

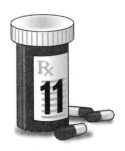

TO INTUBATE OR NOT TO INTUBATE: HOUSE'S PRINCIPLES AND PRIORITIES

Barbara Anne Stock and Teresa Blankmeyer Burke

The Principles

In the episode "DNR," House intubates a patient, John Henry Giles, against Giles's wishes. House's team members, Foreman in particular, object:

> Foreman: You tubed him and he didn't wanna be tubed! He has a legal paper saying just that.

> House: To intubate or not to intubate, that is the big ethical question. Actually, I was hoping we could avoid it, maybe just practice some medicine.

House, of course, is able to diagnose and cure Giles, so everything turns out for the best. But that doesn't negate the fact that he basically assaulted a patient, sticking equipment into the man's throat without his permission. Was this action immoral? This "big ethical question" arises out of the conflict between two ideals that, taken separately, both seem correct: (1) Doctors should do what is best for their patients, and (2) Patients have the right to control what happens to their own bodies. Resolving such a dilemma involves prioritizing, deciding which ideal is more important in a given situation. Here we find ourselves in the realm of bioethics, the area of philosophy that includes ethical analysis of medical decisions.

Principlism, a well-known bioethical approach, reduces ethical behavior to the following rules: don't harm anyone, help people, let people make their own decisions, and be fair. Bioethicists often refer to these rules as the principles of non-maleficence, beneficence, autonomy, and justice.[1] Many of the best "I can't believe he did that!" moments on the show occur when House gleefully flouts these principles.

Nonmaleficence, the oldest of the principles, is often attributed to the ancient medical precept of *primum non nocere*, or *first, do no harm*. This principle can be interpreted strictly (never cause harm) or modestly (play it safe, harm only when clearly medically necessary). A doctor who was committed to *never* causing harm would not, for example, amputate a limb infected with flesh-eating bacteria, while a doctor who adopted the modest approach would see the harm of amputation as justified. House's plan to harvest a spinal nerve from his CIPA patient who couldn't feel pain, a procedure that was not diagnostically necessary and might cause paralysis, violates both interpretations of this principle ("Insensitive"). (CIPA is an acronym for "congenital insensitivity to pain with anhidrosis.")

Where nonmaleficence requires people simply to avoid harm, beneficence requires people to take action and help. House tends to abide by the principle of beneficence, but the clinic patient with a cockroach in his ear might have hoped for a more prompt application of this principle. To avoid clinic duty, House paralyzed the patient and went through a fictitious differential diagnosis before removing the roach ("One Day, One Room").

Autonomy, the principle of respect for persons, says that people should be able to control their own lives. Doctors cannot simply decide what they think is best for their patients and do it. Rather, they must explain the options and abide by the patient's decision, a process called *informed consent*. Clearly, when House intubates Giles in "DNR," he overrides the patient's autonomy.

Justice, the principle of fairness, requires that health care goods be distributed equally and without undue burden to any party. Naturally, this becomes complicated when people's needs differ. The principle of justice only encourages the fair distribution of resources; it does not spell out *how* these resources should be divvied up. As an illustration of justice, or lack thereof, consider this discussion regarding the MRI machine, which House and his team have a penchant for breaking, from "Euphoria, Part 1":

> House: Well, it doesn't matter; we obviously can't use it on this patient.
>
> Cameron: No, but there are other doctors in this hospital, and other patients.

A just approach would take the needs of others into consideration.

Beneficence Trumps Nonmaleficence

House's priorities and principles are not always perfectly clear. But one ranking seems evident: House thinks that beneficence is generally more important than nonmaleficence. In "Damned If You Do," House declares that he "wasn't impressed" by the Hippocratic oath and notes that "pretty much all the drugs

I prescribe are addictive and dangerous." In other words, he is quite willing to risk harming patients in order to potentially help them. House not only rejects the strict interpretation of nonmaleficence, but the modest one as well, since he clearly does not play it safe. We've seen him order a colonoscopy on an unsedated patient, wipe out a patient's memories via electroshock, and intentionally make a sick child sicker. Still, ranking beneficence above nonmaleficence does not mean House recklessly harms his patients. In "Distractions," the patient's burns made the usual diagnostic tests too risky, so House and his team sought alternative methods to obtain needed information. But minimizing harm is not his top priority. If potential harms are counterbalanced by potential benefits, House does the procedure.

Beneficence Trumps Autonomy?

When it comes to prioritizing beneficence and autonomy, House is less consistent. Most often, he goes with beneficence, tending to regard the informed consent process as simply another hurdle. Sometimes he blatantly disregards his patients' decisions, such as when he ignored Giles's DNR order in the scene described at the beginning of this chapter, and in "Informed Consent," when he sedated Ezra Powell so that he could perform tests that Powell had explicitly refused. Other times he lies to obtain consent, such as when he told baseball star Hank Wiggen that an antisteroid drug was a calcium supplement—"like milk" ("Sports Medicine"). And, of course, he is not above bullying patients and their family members into agreeing with him or enlisting Wilson's help to manipulate them.

Clearly, House does not regard his patients' autonomy as being of primary importance; that designation is reserved for his patients' *welfare*. House would rather do what is best for his patients, what will really help them, than do what his patients want. Why is there so often such great disparity between what people want and what is best for them? Because people are idiots, of course!

Occasionally, however, House is willing to accept a patient's decision even though he believes it is not really in the patient's best interest. A notable example involves Rebecca Adler in the "Pilot." House figured out that Ms. Adler had a tapeworm in her brain. Though he had no proof of this hypothesis, he would be able to confirm it by a relatively risk-free treatment. Having grown skeptical of House's claims to know what is wrong with her, Rebecca refused treatment, preferring to go home to die. House tried to persuade her, but did not coerce her into treatment even when his team members suggested plans for doing so:

Foreman: Maybe we can get a court order, override her wishes. Claim she doesn't have the capacity to make this decision.

House: But she does.

Cameron: But we could claim that the illness made her mentally incompetent.

Foreman: Pretty common result.

House: That didn't happen here.

Wilson: He's not gonna do it. She's not just a file to him anymore. He respects her.

Cameron: So because you respect her, you're going to let her die?

House: I solved the case, my work is done.

Is there something that distinguishes Rebecca from other patients, or is House just being arbitrary? Wilson's explanation that House respects Rebecca is inadequate. House apparently respected Giles and Powell as much as he respects any patient, yet he overturned their decisions.

House does have a consistent ethical position, but it is one that depends on an idiosyncratic view of informed consent. Medical personnel obtain informed consent by explaining the treatment options and letting patients decide which to accept. This process can go awry in at least two ways: the *consent* itself could be not genuine, such as when a patient is coerced, or the information the patient is given could be inaccurate or incomplete, rendering the patient's decision not truly *informed*. House's idiosyncratic view is that a patient is not fully informed until he or she has the benefit of House's diagnosis. Ezra Powell had no diagnosis. Since he did not know what was wrong with him, his decision to die was uninformed. John Henry Giles had a diagnosis of ALS from another doctor, but House believed this diagnosis was wrong. So Giles's consent to the DNR order was *mis*informed and, therefore, invalid. Rebecca, on the other hand, had all the information that House could give her. Thus, the key difference between Powell and Giles versus Rebecca Adler is summarized in the last line of the dialogue: "I solved the case, my work is done."

In addition to his unique criterion for when consent is truly informed, House also seems to have a low regard for what we might call "proxy consent"—one person giving consent for another. The ethical and legal justification for proxy consent is as follows: Each person has the right to accept or refuse medical intervention. A person who is incompetent to accept or refuse (for example, an infant or a comatose person) does not thereby forfeit this right. Instead, another person, usually a family member, may exercise this right on the incompetent person's behalf. The job of this proxy consenter is to try to act as they believe the incompetent patient would act, were he or she able.

House may be suspicious of this process because he saw it go so badly astray in his own case. Stacy, House's medical proxy, did not act as he would have with regard to excising damaged tissue from his leg ("Three Stories"). Even when a proxy doesn't act directly counter to the patient's expressed wishes, those wishes may be unknowable—for example, in the case of someone who never communicated her wishes, or a newborn who hasn't the cognition to *have* wishes. So proxy consent often amounts to the proxy deciding what he or she thinks is best for the patient. House, ever aware of people's ulterior motives and capacity for self-deception, is unconvinced that family members know what is best for each other. One notable exception to this attitude occurred in "Half-Wit," when House placed the decision to remove the damaged half of a musical savant's brain squarely in the patient's father's hands. In this case, the father really did seem better equipped than anyone else (including House) to determine what would be good for his son.

Beneficence Trumps Justice?

Okay, so far we've seen House rank beneficence over non-maleficence and (usually) beneficence over autonomy. What about justice? Real-world questions of justice typically involve problems of distributing limited resources. In *House*'s world, resources are almost always plentiful; nobody spares a thought for the economics of maintaining a team of four doctors who treat only a handful of patients each month, ordering many expensive tests for each one. Nobody, that is, except hospital board chairman Edward Vogler. Unfortunately for proponents of health care justice, Vogler's role on the show was to serve as a nemesis for House rather than as a means of examining inequities in the use of health care resources.

When, on rare occasions, House concerns himself with the financial side of health care, he seems willing to work the system for those who are truly in need. Yet he is impatient with people who consume more than their share of resources—"free riders." The first of these complementary tendencies is shown in "Failure to Communicate," where we learn that House has been prescribing Medicaid-covered drugs for atypical uses (such as Viagra for a heart condition) so that his patients get what they need. In "The Mistake," we see the second tendency: House scares a young man, who has expensive electronic toys but lacks health insurance, into getting insured. House's scorn for the patient may be exacerbated by the fact that the patient is using a resource—free clinic time—that could better be used by those who need it more.

Most attention to resource allocation on *House* isn't focused on the hospital budget or health insurance (not really compelling television!), but deals with a more dramatically engaging limited resource: donated organs. The principle of justice maintains that resources should be distributed fairly. "Fairly" does not mean randomly, however. One *could* assign donated organs through a lottery system, or on a strictly first-come, first-served basis, but these methods would not necessarily provide organs to the patients who need them the most. So what would be fair? Philosopher John Rawls (1921–2002) suggests that we can test systems for fairness by asking ourselves whether a reasonable person would endorse the system *if she didn't know what her status would be.*[2] Imagine that you might need an organ at some point in your life, but you don't know anything about your social, economic, or health circumstances. What kind of system would you want to have in place? You would probably opt for a system where (1) patients with the most urgent needs get priority, (2) wealth and social status are irrelevant, and (3) patients who are likely to have successful outcomes get priority over those likely to die anyway. The Princeton-Plainsboro Teaching Hospital strives to implement just such a fair system. When allocating organs, the distribution committee considers both patient health needs and patient behavior.[3] Some conditions, such as disease induced by untreated or unresolved patient behavior, automatically exclude the patient from qualifying for organ transplants, since these conditions reduce the chances of long term successful outcomes. Thus, a Vicodin addict—like House himself—would unlikely be given another liver to destroy.

Twice in the series we see House fighting for his patients to get organs. When Carly, a bulimic high-powered business executive, is diagnosed with severe congestive heart failure as a result of taking ipecac to induce vomiting, House goes to the transplant committee to advocate for her ("Control"). Knowing that Carly's prior behavior disqualifies her for a heart transplant, House lies to the committee in order to save her life, prioritizing beneficence over justice. We will never know whether House's lie resulted in another transplant candidate— one who met the full transplant criteria—dying because of the lost opportunity to gain a heart. In "Sex Kills," House does not go so far as deceiving the transplant committee to get a heart for his elderly patient, Henry, but he does make it clear that his role is to look out for his patient's interests, not necessarily what is fair in the big picture. After Henry is turned down, the following exchange takes place:

> Cameron: I wrote a letter to the board of directors appealing the transplant committee's decision. I'm alleging bias against you clouded their medical judgment. I need you to sign.
>
> House: They made the right call.
>
> Cameron: You don't believe that. You told the committee—
>
> House: I was advocating for my patient. [he signs the letter anyway]
>
> Cameron: Then why are you—
>
> House: Advocating for my patient . . .

Interestingly, while in both of these cases House's actions come down on the side of beneficence rather than justice, in both cases House displays uncharacteristic doubts. In the first case, he actually goes to the patient's room to assure himself that Carly really wants to live, and in the second he directly admits that the committee made the right call. This could indicate that House has reservations about subordinating justice to beneficence, but we think House's view is subtler than that: he holds that even if justice should take precedence, it is not his role to facilitate that. In other words, he thinks a doctor's role is to help *his* patients, not worry about what is most fair for all patients.

Evaluation: Doing the Math

Is House right to be unimpressed with the principle of non-maleficence? Perhaps a better way to put this question is, "How conservative should doctors be about risking harm?" Nonmaleficence, even in its modest (and, we believe, more plausible) interpretation, says to play it safe. Even one who is quite risk-averse will accept a small amount of harm if it brings about great benefits, and will accept a small chance of serious harm if it brings a great chance of benefit. Few would object to vaccinations, for example, though they directly cause a small amount of harm (pain) and confer a very low risk of serious harm (death). But a conservative balks at risks beyond such minimal levels.

House takes risks well beyond those tolerated by the conservative approach; he is *not* risk-averse. Not only is he willing to accept minor harms or minuscule chances of major harm, he orders procedures that carry serious risk for serious harm. In "Autopsy," for instance, he actually kills his young patient (albeit temporarily!) in order to save her life. Of course, he puts patients through these procedures in the hope that they will receive great benefits from them: they will be diagnosed and cured. And he gets results. His methods may be unorthodox, but they save patients' lives—lives that would likely be lost using a more conservative approach.

Doing what gets the best overall results is the basis of the ethical theory known as utilitarianism, which instructs us to perform actions that will bring about the best possible long-term consequences for everyone involved. This theory will sometimes recommend doing harm, for example, if doing so allows one to achieve a greater good or avoid a greater harm. This aspect of utilitarianism gives many people pause. It's easy to come up with horror stories about actions a utilitarian might endorse, such as killing a homeless person and distributing his organs among four people who need transplants, with the rationale that four living people is a better consequence than one living person. In reality, however, a prudent utilitarian would be wary of such actions. Whacking vagrants for their body parts is likely to cause unintended negative results, such as widespread distrust of the health care system.

At least with regard to his patients, House is the best utilitarian on television since Mr. Spock. As he proclaimed in "Detox," "I take risks, sometimes patients die. But not taking risks causes more patients to die, so I guess my biggest problem is I've been cursed with the ability to do the math." House's "doing the math" with his patients' lives can come off as cold and calculating, but it provides a viable defense for his stance on nonmaleficence: being willing to harm patients leads to the best overall results.

With regard to House's prioritizing beneficence over autonomy, we saw that he tends to be swayed by patients' autonomous decisions only if their consent is informed to his satisfaction, and that he is not satisfied until he has given his diagnosis. This standard is, to put it delicately, completely nuts. It would mean that patients are totally at House's mercy until he knows what is wrong with them—they choose to seek his help, and they choose whether to accept treatment after the diagnosis, but in between those times House makes all the decisions! Of course, Cuddy would never stand for this, nor should she. Even House probably realizes that having to justify diagnostic procedures to patients and their families is pragmatically useful. Dealing with their resistance can prompt him to think of better ways to get the information he needs.

Still, House's notion of informed consent does raise important questions about this crucial concept. Assuming we reject the "You're not informed until House says you are" criterion, how much information *is* sufficient? Foreman, seeking consent for a procedure, tells the parents of a patient, "Look, I'm sorry, I can explain this as best I can, but the notion that you're gonna fully understand your son's treatment and make an informed decision is . . . kinda insane. Now, here's what you need to know, it's dangerous, it could kill him, you should do it" ("Paternity"). Can we honestly expect patients and their families to understand enough to make informed decisions? Foreman is on the right track when he zeros in on the risks (though one hopes he gave a bit more detail offscreen!). Decision makers don't need to understand all of the science involved, but they do need to understand what could go wrong and how likely it is that things will go wrong. Even providing that, however, raises questions about how much information is enough. Should patients be informed, for example, about their physician's or their hospital's success rate with the particular procedure being offered? For a statistically sophisticated patient, this information might be relevant; for others it would simply add to the overwhelming confusion.

What about House's view that doctors should function as advocates for their patients, rather than concerning themselves with overall justice? In the real world, the role of physicians as patient advocates is juxtaposed with administrators defending their obligation to budget institutional resources fairly. We don't see much of this latter role on *House*. Even though House and Cuddy frequently clash over House's extreme methods of diagnosing patients, Cuddy rarely wields the administrative budget card. Still, it seems like an appropriate division of labor. The thought of doctors "rationing at the bedside" is chilling, yet somebody has to make sure there are enough resources to go around. The problem with removing frontline doctors from such concerns is that doing so removes some of the best potential advocates for change in the way that health care is provided. With regard to decisions about who gets transplantable organs, the distribution system is designed to provide organs to the patients who are most likely to die without them and most likely to live with them. Given his utilitarian tendencies, House ought to agree with this system. Yet it is hard to blame him for trying to thwart the system in favor of his own patients.

Diagnosis

House likes to break rules, disregarding dress codes, speed limits, basic etiquette, and even bioethical principles. His ethical priorities are often controversial, and his decisions are sometimes frankly outrageous. But he tends to have surprisingly coherent, cogent reasons behind what he does.

Although neither of the authors of this chapter would like to have House as her personal physician, we wouldn't mind serving with him on an ethics committee. Just imagine what kind of bet House would have to lose to get him to do such a thing . . .

NOTES

1. Tom L. Beauchamp and James F. Childress, *Principles of Biomedical Ethics*, 5th ed. (Oxford: Oxford Univ. Press, 2001).

2. John Rawls, *A Theory of Justice* (Cambridge, MA: Harvard Univ. Press, 1971), 16.

3. Decisions about who gets transplantable organs don't happen the way they are shown on *House*. Organ transplantation is not a matter of internal hospital politics but is centralized through a federally subsidized program, the United Network for Organ Sharing (UNOS). (http://www.unos.org/).

HOUSE AND MEDICAL PATERNALISM: "YOU CAN'T ALWAYS GET WHAT YOU WANT"

Mark R. Wicclair

In the closing scene of the season one finale, "Honeymoon," we hear Mick Jagger sing, "You can't always get what you want, but if you try sometimes, you might find, you get what you need." These words express a recurrent paternalistic theme of the series: patients don't always get what they *want* (their preferences and choices are disregarded), but they get what House believes they *need* (tests, medical procedures, and medications that enable him to successfully diagnose and treat their medical conditions). House routinely practices paternalism, deciding what is best for patients without their consent.

House and the Concept of Paternalism

Paternalism is clearly against the norms of mainstream medical ethics. Informed consent—the principle that, except in emergency situations, medical interventions require the *voluntary* and *informed* consent of patients or their surrogates—is a core ethical principle in health care.[1] A corollary of informed consent is that patients who are able to decide for themselves have a right to refuse treatment recommendations. Another core principle is that when patients lack decision-making capacity, surrogates should make decisions in line with the wishes and values of the patient. Both of these principles reflect a strong opposition to paternalism in contemporary medical ethics.

House believes that he knows what is best for his patients, and he repeatedly flouts their wishes in order to diagnose and treat their illnesses. For him, informed consent is a meaningless ritual and, worse yet, a potential obstacle to providing patients the tests, medical procedures, and medications that he believes they *need*. For House, the end—restoring the health of patients— justifies the means, which include disregarding patient preferences, coercion, withholding information, deception, lying, and even breaking and entering into patients' homes. These means are paternalistic insofar as: (1) the aim is to promote the *good of patients* rather than the interests of others (for example, House or Princeton-Plainsboro Hospital), and (2) the *patient* is the person who is subject to coercion, deception, and so forth.

"Honeymoon" illustrates the importance of the first condition. In that episode, a patient named Mark refuses to allow House to perform a diagnostic test. Mark, the husband of Stacy, House's former fiancée, is completely paralyzed. House believes he knows the cause of Mark's symptoms, acute intermittent porphyria (AIP). To confirm the diagnosis, House proposes to trigger a seizure with an injection and then perform a test on a urine sample. Triggering seizures is risky, and Mark refuses. However, at Stacy's urging, House carries out his recommended plan despite the protests of Mark and each of the three members of the medical team (Cameron, Chase, and Foreman). Performing the tests against Mark's wishes is an instance of paternalism only if House's primary goal was to *benefit Mark* (by diagnosing and treating his illness). It would *not* qualify as paternalism if House's primary goal had been to enhance his reputation and receive a promotion or win back Stacy by acceding to her pleas for him to proceed with the test.

In the series, House is portrayed as a physician who, despite his rude and insulting behavior, is committed to promoting the health of his patients. Paradoxically, despite his horrible bedside manner, he is willing to do almost anything to see to it that patients get the tests and treatments that he believes they need. So when we see House employ means such as deception and coercion to ensure that patients receive tests and therapeutic measures, absent evidence to the contrary, viewers can assume that his actions satisfy the first condition of paternalism.

Such deception and coercion, however, can be classified as paternalism only when the second condition is satisfied as well—only when the *patient* is deceived or coerced. This condition is satisfied by House in "Need to Know" when he gets a patient to admit to taking her daughter's Ritalin by deceiving her into believing that a cafeteria menu is a positive toxicology screen report. This is an instance of paternalistic deception insofar as the patient was deceived and the aim of tricking her into revealing information she did not want to disclose was to enable House to promote her well-being by diagnosing and treating her condition. Frequently, however, when House relies on deception to enable him to diagnose and treat patients' medical conditions, it is directed at people *other* than the patient (for example, other health professionals or family members) and therefore does not qualify as paternalism.

This point can be illustrated by comparing scenes from two season one episodes, "Poison" and "Love Hurts." In "Poison," House believes that a teenager's symptoms are caused by pesticide poisoning. If this diagnosis is correct, the indicated treatment is the pesticide hydrolase. However, the boy's mother refuses to consent when she learns the recommended treatment could be harmful if the diagnosis is wrong. To get the mother to consent, House reads her a release form that uses provocative language, including the statements "It is not the hospital's fault if my son kicks off," and "I understand my doctors consider my decision to be completely idiotic." With the aid of these tactics, House succeeds in getting the boy's mother to sign a consent form for the pesticide hydrolase. In "Love Hurts," a patient named Harvey Park has an ongoing relationship with a dominatrix. When Harvey refuses recommended surgery, Chase, simulating the role of a dominatrix, tries to pressure Harvey into consenting. When this tactic fails, Harvey's dominatrix is enlisted to order him to agree to surgery. The tactics used in both "Poison" and "Love Hurts" may well cross the line that separates "persuasion" from "undue pressure and influence." However, only in the latter case is it appropriate to classify the tactics as *paternalistic* because it is only in that case that they are applied to the *patient*. Whereas attempting to override patients' choices for their own good is paternalistic, attempting to override parental choices for the good of their children is not.[2]

The Presentation of Medical Paternalism in the Fictional World of *House*

As to be expected, the series provides viewers with several reasons for deciding in favor of House's assessment of medical paternalism. Time after time, when he gives patients what he believes they need rather than what they want, the outcome appears to be better for the patient than it would have been if the patient had received what he or she wanted. Accordingly, a recurrent message appears to be that doctors—or at least Dr. House—do indeed know what is best for patients, and the good outcomes for patients justify medical paternalism. This message is reinforced when patients acknowledge that they benefited from medical paternalism. Most are pleased with the good outcome and express no anger or resentment. Some even express gratitude.

In "Honeymoon," the test House performed despite Mark's protests confirms the suspected diagnosis, and House orders the indicated treatment. We later see Mark, who is no longer paralyzed, jokingly ask Stacy whether she wants to arm-wrestle. They are both very happy, and Mark does not criticize House's failure to respect his wishes. Mark's only comment about House is "He's still a maniac." The Rolling Stones song at the end of the episode drives home the paternalistic message that giving patients what they need is more important than giving them what they want.

In "DNR," contrary to the patient's stated wishes, House resuscitates and performs tests on a paralyzed horn player named John Henry Giles. Two years earlier a prominent physician had diagnosed the cause of the paralysis as ALS. However, House refuses to accept that diagnosis, and he determines the actual diagnosis and orders the indicated treatment. At the end of the episode, as John Henry walks out of the hospital, he meets House and says, "Thanks for sticking with the case." If House had respected John Henry's wishes, he would be dead rather than walking out of the hospital. Once again, it appears that House knows best, and medical paternalism prevented an unnecessary and premature death, a result for which the patient is grateful.

A particularly powerful endorsement of medical paternalism occurs in "Three Stories," an episode in which House himself is on the receiving end. While giving a lecture to medical students, House refers to his own past experience as a patient, and we see the events he describes in a flashback. He is in severe pain due to muscle necrosis in his leg. Cuddy, who currently is a hospital administrator, was his physician then. She recommends an amputation, claiming it is necessary to save his life, but House refuses. He is willing to risk dying in order to have a chance of regaining full use of his leg, and he wants to be put in a temporary drug-induced coma for relief of pain. After House loses consciousness, Stacy, his fiancée at the time, asks Cuddy to perform a procedure that is expected to give House a better chance of surviving. Both know that House does not want the procedure, but it is performed with Stacy's approval. He receives the treatment that Stacy and Cuddy believe he needs rather than the treatment he wants. He survives the surgical procedure that was performed contrary to his wishes, and an amputation was not necessary. However, he suffers severe chronic pain and cannot walk without a cane. Despite this somewhat mixed result, an exchange among three medical students and House at the end of the lecture appears to endorse the decision to override House's wishes:

House: Because of the extent of the muscle removed, the utility of the patient's [House's] leg was severely compromised. Because of the time delay in making the diagnosis, the patient continues to experience chronic pain.

First Medical Student: She [Stacy] had no right to do that.

Second Medical Student: She had the proxy.

First Medical Student: She knew he didn't want the surgery.

Second Medical Student: She saved his life.

Third Medical Student: We don't know that; maybe he would have been fine.

First Medical Student: It doesn't matter. It's the patient's call.

Second Medical Student: The patient's an idiot.

House: They usually are.

True to form, House's negative assessment of the intelligence of patients is provocative and exaggerated. Nevertheless, it affirms the paternalistic conclusion that patients, including even House himself, don't know what they need.

There are a few episodes in which paternalism is resisted and patients are given what they want rather than what House or another member of the medical team believes they need. In these episodes, however, the rejection of paternalism is presented as a questionable decision. For example, in "Forever," a hospitalized young woman named Kara kills her infant son Michael. The team determines that she has pellagra, which explains her hallucinations and the voices that urged her to kill Michael. Celiac disease, which is the cause of Kara's pellagra, also caused cancer of her stomach lining. She is guilt-ridden for killing Michael, but House attempts to persuade her that due to her pellagra-induced psychosis, she is not responsible for Michael's death. He tells her, "This is not your fault. . . . You do not deserve to die." House, however, fails to convince Kara, and she refuses treatment by responding, "I don't want to live." In the next scene, which begins with House reporting Kara's decision to Foreman, we observe the following exchange:

House: She said no.

Foreman: So we get her declared unstable, appoint a medical power . . .

House: She was unstable. Now she's sane. She's entitled to refuse treatment.

Foreman: You have to change her mind, you can't just walk away.

Ironically, although House does "walk away," this may be a case in which the patient's current wishes should not have been honored. She may not be "insane," but she clearly is emotionally distraught, and her thinking and judgment may be impaired as a result. At the very least, viewers might well agree with Foreman that other options should have been explored before honoring Kara's wishes and walking away.

The Ethics of Medical Paternalism in the Real World

Although the case for medical paternalism in the fictional world of *House* may seem to be compelling, the appropriateness of the practice in the real world remains questionable. In many respects, the fictional world of *House* is a fantasy. By the end of each episode, House and his team usually have successfully identified and treated the patient's illness. Unfortunately, in the real world, diagnoses and prognoses are significantly more elusive, and there are many chronic, untreatable, and terminal diseases. For example, in "Honeymoon," House's diagnosis was correct, and Mark received the medically indicated treatment and was well on the road to recovery by the end of the episode. But in the real world, a physician's diagnosis might have been mistaken, and the test that House administered against Mark's wishes might have killed him. In "DNR," House's belief that John Henry does not have ALS is confirmed, and surgery reverses his paralysis. In the real world, however, the other physician's diagnosis might have been correct, and the patient might have been subject to pointless tests and interventions that increased his discomfort and thwarted his desire to die with dignity. Surely viewers would be less inclined to accept House's paternalistic actions if Mark had died as a result of the test or if it did not confirm House's diagnosis, or if John Henry did have ALS. Yet both outcomes were distinct possibilities at the time each decision was made.

In the real world of medicine, when decisions are made about tests and therapies, the outcome is unknown. At best, probabilities can be assigned to various outcomes and the potential benefits and harms associated with each. Accordingly, the medical paternalism of House and his team should be assessed at the time when a decision has to be made, based on what is known at the time, and not after the fact, when the outcome is known.

In the world of *House*, patients are usually grateful after House disregards their wishes and succeeds in diagnosing and treating their illnesses. In real life, however, patients are not always so forgiving when doctors disregard their preferences and choices. To see this, let's compare the reactions of Mark and John Henry, who were pleased and appreciative, to the reaction of an actual patient, Donald (Dax) Cowart, who was subject to medical interventions against his wishes.[3]

In 1973, at the age of twenty-five, Dax suffered severe burns over much of his body as a result of a propane gas explosion. In spite of his persistent and repeated protests and a psychiatrist's finding that he was competent, Dax was forced to undergo extremely painful burn treatments. He survived, but he was blind and badly scarred, he lost the use of his arms, and his fingers had to be amputated. Ultimately, Dax was satisfied with his quality of life. However, he remained angry that his wishes were not respected, and he became an advocate for patient rights, in particular the right to refuse medical treatment.

Why, it might be asked, is Dax angry and resentful? After all, he admits that he is enjoying life, and but for the medical paternalism of his doctors, he would be dead. In a documentary about him entitled *Dax's Case*,[4] he offers two reasons. First, he believes that the means (the excruciating pain and extreme suffering associated with the burn treatments that he endured for months) did not justify the end (preventing his death). Accordingly, Dax says that even if he knew the outcome would be the same, if he had to make the choice again, he would still refuse treatment. Second, he says he values freedom and the ability to choose for himself. Accordingly, he is angry that others (his mother and physicians) decided for him.

Dax's first reason helps to expose a fallacy in the notion that a brilliant clinician such as House knows what is best for patients. Due to their medical training and expertise, physicians may know best how to keep their patients alive. However, keeping a patient alive will not necessarily promote the patient's good or best interests. When there are treatment options (nontreatment is always one option), determining which is best *for a particular patient* (*evaluating* the potential benefits and harms) depends on that patient's distinctive preferences and values. As a popular saying puts it, "Different strokes for different folks." For Dax, but not necessarily for all patients in a similar situation, avoiding the pain and suffering associated with burn treatments was more important than preventing death. Accordingly, even though the outcome in his case was good, it cannot be said that treating him against his wishes promoted his best interests better than forgoing treatment would have.

Dax's case also challenges the recurrent notion in the series that medical paternalism is justified because House and his team provide patients what they *need*. What do patients need? House's answer is health and longevity. But, as Dax illustrates, patients can have various goals and values other than health or longevity. Dax valued freedom and the absence of pain, and he assigned higher priority to both than to health and longevity. As House himself illustrates in "Three Stories," patients can value bodily integrity more than life, as shown by the fact that they are willing to bear an increased risk of death in order to keep a limb or breast or in order to reduce the risk of incontinence, sterility, or impotence. Dr. Ezra Powell, a patient in the season three episode "Informed Consent," who was subjected to medical interventions he did not want, placed a very high value on death with dignity. In "The Right Stuff," a pilot named Greta values flying so much that she does not want to undergo tests or treatments that might save her life but also result in the Air Force's permanently grounding her. Clearly, then, although patients may need certain medical interventions to stay alive, it does not follow that they need those interventions to promote their good (the goals that matter most to them).

Even when limited to considerations of health, it is mistaken to think that there always are objective standards for ascertaining patients' needs. In "Honeymoon," did Mark *need* the test that House recommended? If health is the exclusive goal, and the test is the only effective means to restore his health, House might plausibly claim that he needed it. But in the real world, the situation is much more complex. Tests have potential benefits as well as risks, and forgoing tests also has potential benefits as well as risks. In Mark's case, the test *might* provide a decisive diagnosis of his illness, but it also might not. It might cause a further deterioration in his health or even lead to his death. Even if the test leads to a correct diagnosis, the treatment may not be effective. On the other hand, without the test, Mark *might* die, but his health also might not worsen or it might even improve. House might be wrong, and the correct diagnosis might be discovered, or there might be a spontaneous remission. There is no "objective" standard for weighing all of these potential benefits and harms and determining whether the potential benefits of the test House recommended outweigh the risks. Accordingly, there is no "objective" right answer to the question "Does Mark need the test?" The answer to this question requires value judgments, and Mark's answer may or may not be the same as House's or another patient's.

In the world of *House*, choices typically are a matter of life or death: If a patient doesn't receive a certain medical intervention, he or she will die. In the real world, however, choices are not always so stark. Decisions about back, knee, bunion, deviated septum, or prostate surgery, or medication for severe acne and countless others are not life-or-death choices. In such cases, patients must weigh the potential benefits and risks and determine whether the probability and the amount of the potential benefits are high enough to outweigh the risks. If, after careful consideration, a patient concludes that she does not want the procedure, it would be unwarranted for a physician to insist that the patient *needs* it.

Dax's second reason for his anger and resentment is connected with an important concept, autonomy, and a corresponding ethical principle, respect for autonomy, which provides the basis for another challenge to the medical paternalism practiced by House and his team. Even if they effectively diagnose and treat a patient's illness, when they disregard the patient's choices, they fail to respect the patient's autonomy, which can have a significant moral cost. The value of autonomy is confirmed by a thought experiment proposed by the late philosopher Robert Nozick.[5] Imagine there is an "experience machine," a device that can be connected to people's brains that will produce experiences that make them feel happy. For example, if bowling a 300, winning on *American Idol,* owning a Lamborghini, and receiving a full scholarship from Harvard Law School are experiences that will make a person happy, the experience machine can be programmed to produce those experiences. What would be missing is a sense of *agency.* Insofar as the machine has produced those experiences, the person has not exercised her autonomy. The person has done and accomplished nothing. The medical paternalism practiced by House and his team may make patients happy in the end, but like the experience machine, it does not enable them to exercise their autonomy. The experience machine and Dax serve to remind us that people may value the ability to exercise their autonomy more than happiness.

We can hope that most physicians do not share House's view that patients usually are "idiots." But respect for autonomy may on occasion require a physician to honor a decision that is perceived to be a "mistake" or a "bad" choice. Freedom to make decisions only if they are "correct" or "good" is no real freedom and does not enable patients to exercise their autonomy. Accordingly, it might be said that a price of the exercise of autonomy is the risk of making bad decisions, and like Dax, many people are willing to pay this price.

The many reasons for challenging medical paternalism in the real world support a strong presumption against it.

However, it would be unwarranted to conclude that medical paternalism is *never* ethically justified. When evaluating paternalism, it is important to distinguish between cases in which agents are fully autonomous and capable of making decisions for themselves, on the one hand, and cases in which agents lack decision-making capacity or their reasoning ability is deficient or impaired, on the other hand.[6] Accordingly, the antipaternalistic stance of mainstream medical ethics applies to autonomous adults, but not to infants, young children, or adults with severe mental retardation or advanced dementia. Moreover, autonomous persons can suffer temporary diminished autonomy as a result of illness, medication, accidents, or traumatic life events. A previously described scene from "Forever" illustrates this point. Even if House is correct to proclaim that Kara is no longer "insane," it is likely that her thinking and judgment are temporarily impaired, and there is good reason to question whether acceding to her stated wishes will promote her enduring goals and values.

Generally, the case for rebutting the presumption against medical paternalism is strongest when it is undertaken to prevent harm to the patient, and the standard of harm is based on the *patient's* standards of harm and benefit rather than on the standards of others (for example, physicians or family members). Other relevant factors to consider include the magnitude of the expected harm to the patient, the probability that the harm will occur in the absence of paternalistic intervention, whether the expected harm is imminent, whether there are alternative means to prevent the harm, and the likelihood that the contemplated paternalistic intervention will prevent the expected harm. In some situations, these criteria may provide an unambiguous answer. In other situations, however, it may be possible for reasonable people to disagree. House's experience as a patient in "Three Stories" and the significantly different responses of the three medical students may well exemplify a case of this kind. In any event, real-world physicians cannot justify medical paternalism by maintaining simply that patients are "idiots." Determining whether medical paternalism in the real world is ethically justified calls for considerably more nuanced reflection and ethical analysis than is evidenced in the fictional world of *House*.

NOTES

1. See Tom L. Beauchamp and James F. Childress, *Principles of Biomedical Ethics*, 6th ed. (New York: Oxford Univ. Press, 2008); and Ruth R. Faden and Tom L. Beauchamp, *A History and Theory of Informed Consent* (New York: Oxford Univ. Press, 1986).

2. Although not classifiable as paternalism, attempts to override a parent's decision in order to promote a child's well-being are legitimately subject to ethical evaluation.

3. See Lonnie D. Kliever, *Dax's Case: Essays in Medical Ethics and Human Meaning*, (Dallas: Southern Methodist Univ. Press, 1989). Mr. Cowart changed his name from Donald to Dax in 1982.

4. *Dax's Case* was produced by Unicorn Media, Inc., for Concern for Dying, Inc. It was released in 1985.

5. Robert Nozick, *Anarchy, State, and Utopia* (New York: Basic Books, 1974), 42–45.

6. Some philosophers distinguish between "strong" and "weak" paternalism or "extended" and "limited" or "restricted" paternalism. The former type of paternalism is said to occur when it is practiced in relation to autonomous persons, and the latter type of paternalism is said to occur when it is practiced in relation to people who are not fully autonomous. See James F. Childress, *Who Should Decide? Paternalism in Health Care* (New York: Oxford Univ. Press, 1982).

IF THE END DOESN'T JUSTIFY THE MEANS, THEN WHAT DOES?

Catherine Sartin

Thankfully House (almost) never fails to arrive at the correct diagnosis—usually in the last ten minutes of the episode. The outcome of a questionable procedure either provides the key to solving the mystery, or at least provides decisive evidence allowing him to eliminate one or more plausible diagnoses. Still, he is constantly forced to justify his questionable actions to others. In response, we can easily imagine House saying, "If the end doesn't justify the means, then what does?"

What Is a Utilitarian?

With his "end justifies the means" approach, House appears to be acting from utilitarian considerations. Utilitarianism, which was developed by Jeremy Bentham (1748–1822) and John Stuart Mill (1806–1873), holds that the outcome of an action, for all those who will be affected by it, determines whether that action is morally right or wrong. So a utilitarian would consider how a procedure House wants to perform would affect not only the patient and his or her family, but also how it would affect the doctors, the hospital, and future patients. Morally right actions are those that produce good consequences overall; morally wrong actions are those that produce bad consequences overall.

In many cases, this seems to be the way that House reasons about his actions—he justifies them by their good consequences. For example, in "Meaning," House tries to justify giving a cortisol shot to a patient who has been unable to move or communicate for at least six months. House tells Cuddy that if his diagnosis is right, the cortisol shot will give the patient the ability to walk again, hug his child, and dance with his wife; if he is wrong, the shot will not harm the patient in any way. House is clearly trying to justify giving the patient the cortisol shot by its potentially overall good consequences.

Or consider House's reasoning in "Let Sleeping Dogs Lie." A woman, Hannah, is in need of an immediate liver transplant. Her lesbian lover, Max, is a match and a willing donor. The team discovers that prior to becoming ill, Hannah had planned to break up with Max. This presents the team with a dilemma. If they tell Max, she may no longer be willing to be a donor and Hannah will die; if they don't tell Max, both women will live. House reasons that they should not tell because two women alive and in good health are better than only one—even at the cost of some psychological pain. Again, House justifies his actions by claiming that they create the best possible outcome.

Act vs. Rule Utilitarianism

But how should we judge the consequences? "Act utilitarians" hold that we should judge each individual action according to the consequences resulting from that specific action. This allows us to take into account the unique circumstances of each act. It also, however, requires a lot of time and effort. Just imagine trying to decide whether to buy locally grown pears or pears imported from a poor nation. The locally grown pears require less fuel to be consumed because they don't have to travel as far. This is certainly a great benefit to everyone currently on the planet as well as to future generations. However, the farmers of the poor nation may be relying on foreign consumers to buy their products. It might be the only thing keeping them from abject poverty. You would be stopped in your tracks in the middle of the grocery store trying to sort it all out. An act utilitarian would have to consider each individual purchase by itself. She would need to research each type of fruit at each market—where it came from, the plight of those who produced it, and so on—to decide which purchase would produce the best consequences.

This is why some utilitarians, called "rule utilitarians," hold that we should act according to rules or principles that, in general, bring about the best consequences. In the scenario just described, a rule utilitarian would have to base her decision only on whether, in general, reducing carbon emissions or helping those who are impoverished produces the best overall consequences. Once she has made this determination, she can apply her rule to all of her future fruit purchases. This still requires some work, but not nearly as much work as act utilitarianism.

The philosopher Immanuel Kant (1724–1804) had a moral theory similar to rule utilitarianism. Kant (and his followers, called Kantians) also believed we should follow rules, but Kant was not concerned about the consequences of actions. Rather, Kant thought that it is the act itself that is either right or wrong, regardless of the consequences of that act. For instance, Kant maintained that lying is always wrong, even when lying is the only way to save a person's life. He also held that it is never right to treat a person only as a means to an end. For example, it is okay to go to the doctor and make use of his expertise, but it is not okay to treat the doctor as a mere tool, as less than a person.

House favors considering particular circumstances and so tends to reason like an act utilitarian rather than like a rule utilitarian. Consider the episode "Babies and Bathwater." In order to save an expectant mother *and* her unborn child, House must perform an early C-section. This will allow the mother to start a clinical trial for a promising treatment for her small-cell lung cancer, her best hope for long-term survival. Unfortunately, the trial starts well before her due date and the treatment would injure or kill the fetus. On the other hand, an early C-section would lower the baby's chance of survival from nearly 100 percent to 80 percent. House, in his characteristically bad-tempered but honest manner, convinces the patient to have the C-section and start the trial. Meanwhile, he knows that she shouldn't be admitted to the trial since there is a policy that no patient can be admitted to a clinical trial within a month of having a major surgery. The policy is meant not only to protect the patient, but also to protect the integrity of the trial's results. Nonetheless, House gets her into the clinical trial by omitting her current condition and schedules the C-section. (The hospital administration gets wind of his plan before the C-section can be performed and it is canceled at the last minute).

House is clearly considering the unique circumstances of this particular case, reasoning that one participant who is not in compliance with all of the standards will not invalidate the results of the entire study or render them useless. The treatment will pass or fail the trial regardless of how any one patient responds. Furthermore, he is certain that the patient's recent C-section won't cause her any problems. House isn't following a general policy, which, if followed by everyone, would provide the best possible outcome for all the participants and potential recipients of the treatment. Imagine that every physician decided that his or her patient's noncompliance would not alone invalidate the results of the study. If a significant number of patients are admitted by physicians reasoning in this manner, then this overall noncompliance will cause problems for the trial. In fact, this is exactly what the policy is intended to prevent.

A rule utilitarian would follow the policy of not allowing any exceptions because this is the policy that leads to the best consequences when *everyone* follows it. This is also what a Kantian would do, because the alternative involves deceiving the experimenters. When we deceive someone, we are treating that person as merely a means to our own ends, which, as we have already seen, Kantians find unacceptable.

A similar situation arises in "Control." A young female patient is in need of a heart transplant in the immediate future. Normally she would be placed at the top of the list, but House discovers that she suffers from bulimia. Furthermore, her bulimia caused the conditions that have made a new heart necessary. If her disorder is revealed, she will be placed so far down the list that she will almost surely die before receiving a heart—if she is even put on the list at all. After a typically frank conversation with her, House is convinced that she does not want to die and will mend her ways. In light of this he conceals her disorder from the transplant committee (as well as his team). She is placed at the top of the list, receives a new heart, and makes a full recovery.

House clearly brings about the best possible consequences for the patient. She has a new lease on life and is thriving. No one finds out about her disorder until it is too late to remove her from the list. Even then it is not clear, or provable at any rate, that House had prior knowledge of the bulimia. All this means that it is unlikely that the transplant system will suffer any harm. Physicians and patients will not lose faith in the system, and other doctors will not be inspired to follow House's deceitful example. Indeed, House hides the patient's bulimia from his team partly for this reason. But he also hides it from them for a more pragmatic reason: to prevent them from alerting the hospital administration and the transplant committee. After all, not every member of his team reasons like a utilitarian (especially Cameron). In this case, House's reasoning is based entirely on bringing about a certain result, with no concern about treating people as more than a means to an end. Clearly, House is not a Kantian but rather an act utilitarian. His reasoning is based entirely on the particulars of this patient's case.

Best Possible Consequences

Despite his utilitarian reasoning, it is not clear that House actually brings about the best consequences in all cases. Recall the episode "Acceptance," in which an inmate on death row is saved from the poisons in the copier fluid he ingested. During his stay in the hospital it is discovered that he has a tumor situated above his pituitary gland, which may help to explain his sudden rages. Unfortunately, it is unlikely to overturn his conviction, and he is sent back to prison to await his execution. And recall the episode "Lines in the Sand" in which an autistic boy is saved from a nearly fatal parasitic infection only to return to his former, autistic self, leaving his parents to continue to monitor his every move.

Clearly, House is not able to bring about the best *conceivable* consequences in either case. The best *conceivable* consequence doesn't have to be practically possible; it just has to be something we can imagine could (perhaps miraculously) be brought about. The best conceivable consequences in "Acceptance" and "Lines in the Sand" would be to change the inmate's sentence and cure the boy of autism. However, it is not practically possible for House to bring about either of these consequences. The question then becomes whether he brings about the best *possible* consequences.

In the case of the inmate, we must consider whether an extended life (even if it is while incarcerated) is a better consequence than an immediate death. One might think that if the inmate lives, he will have a chance to appeal his sentence and receive a stay of execution. But, as Foreman points out, this is not very likely to happen. One might also reason that it is better because it allows for a better death. If they had refused to treat him, he would have died a painful death. Furthermore, because the tumor wouldn't have been discovered, he would never have had any insight into his own behavior. Of course, this better death does come at the cost of the psychological pain he will endure in the days leading up to his execution. In the end, it may not be clear whether the best possible outcome for the inmate was achieved. Remember, though, that the inmate isn't the only person we have to consider. Preventing his suicide is probably the best possible outcome for those in charge of the prison. It might also be the best for those personally affected by his crimes. They gain insight, just as he does, when the tumor is discovered. It might help to answer some of their questions (such as "How could this happen?") and give them a greater sense of closure and healing.

House thinks that the best possible outcome was achieved. He puts great value on life, at least life in which the person is conscious, aware of surroundings, and so on. Even if you have to live with tremendous pain, he reasons, it is better to be alive. House himself is in constant, unrelenting pain and shows no signs of ever considering suicide. We see his attitude toward life many times throughout the show in his actions toward patients as well. For example, House is vehemently opposed to euthanasia when there is a chance of treatment or a cure. Consider the episode "Informed Consent," in which an aging scientist wants House to help him die. Everyone agrees that the man is in pain and everyone (except House) agrees that he is near death. Only when House determines that the man actually cannot be helped and his (painful) death is imminent does he agree to help him end his life. In order to make this determination, House has to trick the man and run tests against his (explicit) wishes. Others, including Cameron and Chase, don't have the same view of life. They think that it is sometimes reasonable to prefer death over constant, unrelenting pain.

In the case of the autistic boy in "Lines in the Sand," it is clearer that we also need to consider the outcome for those other than the patient. It is practically impossible to know what it is like to have his form of autism. Nonetheless, it is reasonable to suppose that even a life like this is preferable to death. The real difficulty arises in assessing what is better for his parents. If he were to die, this would certainly cause his parents a great deal of pain. On the other hand, it would also allow them to move on with their lives. If he were to survive (as he does), it would mean that they must either continue to give up their lives and care for his every need or put him in an institution. Caring for him is complicated by the fact that he has no emotional attachment to anyone. His parents are not getting any sort of love or even attachment in return for their efforts. This takes a great toll on them. But while putting him in an institution would take the pressure off them, it would also cause them a great deal of emotional anguish.

House seems to think that it would have been better for everyone involved if the boy had died. He thinks that the pain the parents are going through outweighs whatever pleasure the boy gets from being alive. And, it should be mentioned, House doesn't believe the boy has much of a mental life, that he may not in fact take pleasure in being alive. This fits well his general views about life. Consider the way he reasons in "Fetal Position." House doesn't think that the unborn fetus's life (he refuses to call it a baby) should be taken into account when deciding what should be done. He doesn't think its life is valuable, just as he doesn't think the autistic boy's life is valuable. This is not to say that he would support actively killing the boy. It is just to say that he thinks the best possible outcome was not achieved. Wilson, characteristically, takes the other side. He reasons that the boy's death would take a greater emotional toll on the parents than his life is currently taking.

In these particular cases, and probably others as well, House (perhaps) doesn't bring about the best possible consequences. Still, he does bring about the best possible consequences in the majority of cases. As Cuddy says to a skeptical Tritter in season three, "He saves a lot more lives than he loses."

Is House a Morally Good Person?

But is House really interested in bringing about the best possible outcome for everyone involved? Maybe not. The main reason House appeals to the beneficial consequences of a given action is that he knows it will satisfy the person who is asking him to justify the action. House will try to quickly and efficiently knock down any roadblock that is put in his path. If Cuddy were to become focused on the bottom line, House would justify his actions by demonstrating how those actions would save money in the long run. If Wilson were to become focused on advancing medical knowledge, House would justify his actions by showing how those actions would yield new information. It seems that what House is really interested in is solving the puzzle (arriving at a correct diagnosis). It's only incidental that solving this puzzle is almost always beneficial to the patient.

Utilitarians hold that a morally good person is one who tends to bring about the best possible overall consequences. Even if House sometimes misses the mark and even if he acts for selfish reasons, his actions tend to bring about the best possible outcome. Making a mistake or two does not prevent someone from being a morally good person. Even the best among us, Mother Teresa and Gandhi for example, once in a while did something morally wrong. But not acting for the right reasons, with the right intentions, a majority of the time does seem like it might disqualify someone from being a morally good person. Many utilitarians also hold that a good person must not only do the right thing, but do it for the right reasons, with the right intentions.

At first it may seem that House is interested only in helping the patient insofar as it is a way to solve the puzzle. This is clearly not the right reason to want to help the patient, even if helping the patient is the right thing to do. But consider the episode "One Day, One Room." In this episode a rape victim comes to the clinic and is seen by House. There is no puzzle for him to solve. If House was interested only in solving puzzles, he would have refused to talk to her and moved on to the next case. He does initially try to hand the case to someone else, but only because he thinks that he is unqualified to talk to her, not because he isn't interested in talking to her. The patient refuses to talk to anyone else, and after she takes a handful of pills in order to get to see House, he agrees to talk to her. Not only does he talk to her, he actually tries to help her. He has been told that she needs to talk about what happened, and he keeps pushing her to do so. When she tries to direct the conversation away from her rape, he is at a loss for what to do. When he is uncertain how to answer one of her questions, he temporarily puts her under so that he can ask everyone for advice. Time and again, instead of walking away, he tries to help. Eventually she does talk about the rape. Everyone else is quite happy that she is talking about what happened to her; but House is upset that in order to help her, he had to make her cry and relive the rape.

Admittedly, this is only one example of House trying to help a patient without also trying to solve a puzzle. But it is enough to give us pause. Perhaps we should not rush to the judgment that House is a morally bad person. Perhaps he does act for the right reasons, despite all (superficial) appearances to the contrary. Only House really knows.

HOUSE VS. TRITTER: ON THE CLASH OF THEORETICAL AND PRACTICAL AUTHORITY

Kenneth Ehrenberg

In the fifth episode of season three, "Fools for Love," we are introduced to a new character, Michael Tritter, who will play an increasingly important role over the season, albeit in a subplot. Tritter came to the hospital clinic seeking treatment for a rash on his groin that House attributes to dehydration from Tritter's use of nicotine gum (a point of retrospective irony, given Tritter's later persecution of House for his Vicodin addiction). Tritter and House have an argument when House refuses to test his rash, and Tritter responds by kicking House's cane out from under him. House gets back at Tritter by "forgetting" that he left Tritter with a rectal thermometer in his rear end. Later in the episode, House is called in to Cuddy's office to find Tritter there waiting for an apology. When House declines, Tritter replies by saying that he expected as much and that he is really more interested in humiliating House (as House had humiliated him). At the end of the episode, House is pulled over and arrested for possession of narcotics without a prescription. Tritter, it turns out, is a police detective.

As we learn more about Tritter over the course of the next few episodes, we see just how similar he is to House (even spouting the same "Everybody lies" catchphrase). This similarity calls our attention to a philosophical similarity between the two different forms of authority that House and Tritter represent.

Two Kinds of Authority

We are all familiar with two kinds of authority from childhood. One is when someone tells us that we should believe what they say or follow their advice because they know better than we do on some particular subject. This is the form of authority we see on television news shows and in court when an expert is called in to discuss a subject. The other kind of authority is the kind that tells us to do as we are told simply because the person telling us is somehow entitled to control us. This is the kind of authority invoked when a police officer tells us to "move along." Parents of young children are a special combination of both kinds of authority.

House is the consummate authority on medical diagnostics. As such, he represents the form of authority philosophers call "theoretical authority." The reason for this term is quite clear in House's case. The members of House's team help him to perform difficult diagnoses by offering their own theories about what is wrong with a patient. But it is always House who makes the call about which theories are worth testing and which are wrong. He is a theoretical authority in the sense that he is in a position to decide which theories are right and wrong. His authority rests upon the fact that we have good reason to believe what he tells us to believe about what's wrong with us.

Tritter, as a cop who doesn't appear to have any special knowledge (even, we see later, of the law), represents a pure form of the other kind of authority, which philosophers call "practical authority." Such authority is practical in that it claims to control our decisions about what to do and how to act. When Tritter tells House to pull over, he's supposed to pull over just because it is a cop telling him to do so. It is also significant that this authority is frequently backed up with a real or implied threat of one kind or another. If we don't pull over, we'll be arrested and sent to jail. While the threat of punishment may not be strictly necessary for all forms of practical authority, it does appear in the forms we see most commonly: legal authority, parental authority, and workplace authority (where we are supposed to do what the boss says because it is the boss that says so, or else we're fired).

Since the practical authority is actually trying to get us to *do* something, it seems like threats are needed in case we don't do as we are told, especially because we are frequently told to do things that are either against our interest or that we simply don't want to do. On the other hand, when it comes to the advice of a theoretical authority, we are getting better information, usually about what is in our interest (even if only because it's usually in our interest to believe the truth). Theoretical authority is telling us what is true and what to believe; if we don't listen, we have only ourselves to blame.

Patients do what the doctor tells them to do because the implication behind the doctor's direction is that it will help the patient get better. But people also have expectations about how much information a doctor needs to have before drawing a conclusion about the patient's condition. This is what makes House's life so frustrating (and one reason, along with sheer boredom, he hates clinic duty so much). Basically, patients don't realize just how much theoretical authority House has as a result of his vast expertise. He doesn't need to test Tritter's rash because he already knows what it is and how to cure it. But, like so many other patients, Tritter can't believe that any doctor is as good as House and can diagnose the rash without running tests. Of course, his mistrust of House is exacerbated by House's acerbic bedside manner. Patients react to that by thinking that it is House's arrogance that causes him think he knows what's wrong with them rather than his expertise. (In this, House's personality creates its own dissatisfaction by undermining his credibility, forcing him to do more to convince patients of his accuracy.) When it comes to theoretical authority, ultimately, it is still the authority's greater expertise and knowledge that gives a compelling reason for us to listen, agree, and follow advice.

Practical authority figures like Tritter, however, are in a slightly different situation. Sure, they usually have some kind of threat (like jail) to back up their orders; but that can't be enough to *justify* those orders. As the influential twentieth-century legal philosopher H. L. A. Hart pointed out,[1] if the only justification offered for the practical authority is the threat of jail, the law would be no different from a mugging in the street. Hart was responding to the nineteenth-century legal philosopher John Austin, who believed that laws are simply commands backed by the threat of force.[2] Hart noticed that when a mugger points a gun at you and says, "Your money or your life," we usually think that you are under no obligation to give your money; you are simply being forced to do so. Put another way, if you could get away from the situation with both your money and your life, everyone would think you should be congratulated (although perhaps also scolded for taking risks). But we don't usually think that people should be congratulated for getting away with breaking the law (unless we think the law is wrong, or we happen to be in cahoots with the lawbreaker). So something else has to *justify* the law's claim to practical authority.

Authority and Service

This is where the contemporary philosopher Joseph Raz steps in with his service conception of authority.[3] He suggests that the law, or any practical authority, is justified when it gets people who are supposedly subject to that authority to do better at following reasons that already apply to them than they do on their own. In other words, practical authority is justified when we do better by listening to it than by figuring things out on our own. More generally, the claim is that we do better at leading the kinds of lives we want to lead or ought to lead (doing right, avoiding harm, pursuing success, and so on) when we follow the directions of the practical authority. This is clearly the case with parents. Since children are much less aware of the reasons that apply to them (how to do right, how to avoid harm, and so on) than are many adults, the practical authority of parents to direct the behavior of children is generally justified.

One important, although frequently overlooked, aspect of Raz's service conception of authority is that it bases practical authority ultimately upon a certain kind of theoretical authority. If the law's claims to practical authority are justified (which is admittedly a big if), it is likely because the legal officials (including police officers) are in a better position to harmonize people's behavior because of their position as coordinators of social behavior.

When the officer tells you to move along, or not to turn right, the authority she has to do so is based on her being in a better position to know where the roads are closed or where there is greater traffic. The purpose of traffic-directing officers is to coordinate traffic flow in a more efficient way by placing them in strategic locations and to have them direct traffic in those more efficient ways. This, in turn, either gets you to your destination more quickly than if you took the route of your choice, or it gets you to make a small sacrifice in your time so that the majority of people can get to their destinations as quickly as possible. In this second case, one could say that one has a moral reason to make that sacrifice, but without the traffic cop telling you where to go, you wouldn't know how to make that sacrifice. So, according to Raz, legal authority is justified, at least in part, when legal authorities are "experts" in knowing what people have good reasons to do, especially when those people don't know it as well themselves.

A Problem

The problem with this conception of authority arises when certain individuals are more expert than the legal officials. If practical authority is ultimately justified by an appeal to a certain kind of theoretical authority, then that practical authority loses any justification in the face of superior theoretical authority.

One might think that Tritter was just a vindictive cop out for revenge and therefore any authority he had by virtue of his position was not justified. But the picture is slightly more complicated. Tritter said that his pursuit of House was based on his belief that a drug-addicted doctor like House would eventually start harming patients. In essence, Tritter claimed his enforcement of the law was for the good of both House and his patients: House, because it would relieve his addiction, and the patients, because they would have been endangered by House's addiction. In this, the law is arguably written so as to get people to comply better with the reasons that already apply to them. A doctor in House's position would usually have a good reason to stop treating patients. Patients usually have a good reason not to be treated by doctors like House.

What is ignored by Tritter and this analysis is House's practically superhuman expertise, and perhaps the particularities of his field. People turn to House when they cannot get a proper diagnosis by other doctors. House's ability to diagnose difficult cases transcends his Vicodin addiction. This was established all the way back in the first season episode "Detox," when House took a bet from Cuddy to go without Vicodin for a week to show he wasn't addicted. At the time he protested to Cuddy, "The pills don't make me high, they make me neutral." He won the bet but still admitted to Wilson that he was an addict, saying that the pills took away his pain and enabled him to do his job.

His ability to save lives justifies the rejection of the usual thoughts about what would be in patients' interests when confronted by a drug-addicted doctor. Hence House's own theoretical authority undermines the justification of Tritter's practical authority, showing the inherent tension between these two kinds of authority.

Still, there is a similarity in the relationship of each kind of authority to those over whom the authority is exercised. Compared to House, patients are a very ignorant bunch. Compared to Tritter, people are a very powerless bunch and are, furthermore, ignorant of what is in their own best interests when they run afoul of the law. This is highlighted by House and Tritter's shared refrain: "Everybody lies." People lie to both kinds of authority because they are ignorant. People usually lie when they think they are protecting their interests by doing so.

When they are confronted by a theoretical authority like House, they don't realize that for him to provide an accurate diagnosis, he needs complete and accurate information about them and their symptoms. They don't realize it's in their best interest to tell the (whole) truth, thinking that what they withhold or alter could not possibly be relevant. As an example, in the episode "Daddy's Boy," the father of a patient told House and his team that he ran a construction company, expecting it would lead to more favorable treatment for his son than if the doctors knew the truth, which was that he ran a junkyard. It is only after this fact becomes known that House can solve the case (realizing that the patient has radiation poisoning), too late, unfortunately, for the man's son. Of course, this kind of behavior would be very frustrating to a theoretical authority trying to act in the patient's interest. The very person in whose interest the authority is giving advice is undermining its ability to do so.

We are familiar with an analogous situation with legal authorities from any number of police dramas. People lie to the police thinking that by doing so they will protect their privacy or hide minor illicit deeds. What they don't realize is that by doing so, they end up becoming the focus of even more suspicion once the lie is found out. Even when it is the actual culprit of a serious crime who is lying and his guilt is discovered, the fact that he tried to cover up his crime is usually used as a reason to compound the punishment by prosecutors.

But when people are confronted by a practical authority like Tritter, the picture is still slightly more complicated. Practical authority, when justified, does not necessarily mean telling people what is in their individual best practical interest. Instead, it might also be telling them what they have good moral reasons to do. But of course many people would rather pursue their personal practical interests than do the right thing. Practical authorities frequently encounter people who are lying because they prefer to pursue selfish interests.

As the season progresses, Tritter proceeds to pressure Wilson and House's team to give evidence against House. After finding out that House's prescriptions for Vicodin came from Wilson's pad, Tritter freezes Wilson's bank accounts and suspends his prescription privileges. Tritter tries to bribe Foreman by offering a favorable parole hearing and early release for his incarcerated brother. He tries to manipulate Chase into spying on House by reminding him that he did it before (in the first season, for the hospital chairman Vogler), claiming House will assume he's doing it anyway. From Tritter's perspective, these tactics are legally justified to get the information necessary to prosecute House and thereby protect public safety. Since the practical authority supposedly works in the public good, there also appears to be more justification for sacrificing individuals' interests to that important good. The more serious the risk to the public good, the more ready the practical authority might be to sacrifice individuals' interests.

In the case of Wilson, this even extended to sacrificing the interests of his patients. After having his prescription-writing privileges suspended in "Whac-a-Mole," Wilson asked Cameron to write them. Cameron agreed but said she would need to sit in on meetings with his patients since everyone was under Tritter's scrutiny. Cameron's presence causes patients to mistrust Wilson and to suspect he's been making mistakes in their prescriptions. By the end of the episode, Wilson has decided to shut down his practice entirely.

In the conclusion of this subplot ("Words and Deeds"), however, the judge rebukes Tritter for his single-minded pursuit of House by these means. There is a difference between the law and the officials who enforce and implement that law. In essence, the judge understood that Tritter's vendetta and methods of pursuing House were neither in the public interest nor a justified exercise of practical authority. In another way of putting it: Tritter's actions exceeded his mandate. Plainclothes police detectives aren't usually found doing DUI stops. While a detective might have some discretion and latitude in protecting the public interest, that authority is subservient to the judge's, who arguably is in a better position to decide what is really in the public interest and by what means it may be pursued.

The courtroom scene also highlighted the tension between practical and theoretical authority. Cuddy perjures herself in order to save House from being formally charged with drug violations and sent to jail. To this viewer, it seemed pretty clear that the judge suspected that Cuddy was lying. (The judge even commented on House's having some very good friends and hoping that he deserved them.) Normally, if a judge believes that a witness has committed perjury, the judge can threaten the witness with jail unless the witness tells the truth, and the witness can face prosecution for the perjury, regardless. However, it was clear to Cuddy and possibly the judge that House's extraordinary medical expertise (his theoretical authority) justifies trumping the usual rules (the practical authority of the law). So in the end, if this interpretation is correct, the law itself recognized an exception to its authority and that its practical authority must bow to greater theoretical authority. However, any exceptions must be carefully limited or risk undermining the authority of the law as a whole. So, the law grants its exception with a warning attached, voiced by the judge: "Rules and laws apply to everyone. You are not as special as you think."[4]

NOTES

1. H. L. A. Hart, *The Concept of Law* (1961), eds. Penelope A. Bulloch and Joseph Raz, 2nd ed. (Oxford: Clarendon Press, 1994).

2. John Austin, *The Province of Jurisprudence Determined; and, the Uses of the Study of Jurisprudence* (1832), ed. H. L. A. Hart (Indianapolis: Hackett Pub., 1998).

3. Joseph Raz, *The Authority of Law: Essays on Law and Morality* (Oxford; New York: Clarendon Press, 1979); Joseph Raz, *The Morality of Freedom* (Oxford; New York: Clarendon Press, 1986); Joseph Raz, "The Problem of Authority: Revisiting the Service Conception," *Minnesota Law Review* 90 (2006): 1003.

4. Many thanks to Tamar Zeffren and Daniel Friedman for comments and additional episode suggestions, to Sara Morrison of www.televisionwithoutpity.com for compendious and humorous episode plot summaries, and to Celeste Cleary for the link.

PART FOUR

"THE DRUGS DON'T MAKE ME HIGH, THEY MAKE ME NEUTRAL": VIRTUES AND CHARACTER ON *HOUSE*

HOUSE AND THE VIRTUE OF ECCENTRICITY

John R. Fitzpatrick

The fact that *House* has a strong and loyal fan base is not surprising. After all, medical dramas are a television staple and have been popular with both fans and critics alike. Aside from *Grey's Anatomy*, in recent memory one can recall the success of two shows, both of which began in 1994, *Chicago Hope* and *ER*, featuring Dr. Jack McNeil and Dr. Doug Ross. Unlike his predecessors, however, Dr. Gregory House is not a lovable rogue, and his weaknesses are not minor flaws. To use a medical analogy, House is like McNeil or Ross on steroids. So the fact that the fans of *House* like the surly doctor is initially counterintuitive. Why would fans like a fictional character we probably wouldn't like as a real person? Part of the answer must be that we strongly like eccentricity in fictional characters, even though it might be somewhat overwhelming in real life. But a fuller answer must include why we often find eccentrics to be of value generally. Could eccentricity itself be a virtue? I think so, and by examining several eccentric philosophers as well as the work of the nineteenth-century philosopher John Stuart Mill, we will see that this is hardly surprising.

Thoreau and Eccentricity

Henry David Thoreau (1817–1862) is best known for *Walden*, which on one level is a description of two years of his life lived in isolation at Walden Pond. On another level the book is a compelling argument for the claim that the most rational human life is a simple life lived in harmony with nature. In this way Thoreau anticipated much of the modern environmental movement and its focus on sustainable development. Beyond *Walden*, Thoreau's collected works comprise over twenty volumes, and include articulation of his abolitionist stance on slavery and his belief that one has a duty to protest non-violently against laws that one finds unjust. Indeed, Thoreau's nonviolent approach to civil disobedience captured the imagination of many, and clearly was a strong influence on Mahatma Gandhi and Martin Luther King Jr. But Thoreau also wrote in defense of John Brown and his acts of violence, which many people would consider terrorism today.

House, while not marooning himself at Walden Pond, has chosen to lead a life of social isolation. This, in itself, is hardly interesting. But like Thoreau, House seems to be doing it for a reason. It allows him to follow the beat of his own drummer. And while House's acts of refusing to follow normal procedures and standard rules of medical care often strike us as insubordination rather than civil disobedience, occasionally he is willing to put himself at risk on a matter of principle.

For example, in the episode "DNR," House violates a DNR order. Normally, as medicine is practiced in our society, a competent patient has an almost absolute right to refuse medical treatment. Thus, a patient who does not wish invasive or extraordinary measures taken to prolong his or her life can request a DNR—a document in their chart that tells the doctors "Do Not Resuscitate" the patient. House violates the order because he believes that the patient has received a faulty diagnosis from his previous physician, and that if he knew the true state of affairs he would not refuse lifesaving treatment. Ultimately, one has to argue against House's action. After all, there would in practice be no right to refuse treatment if patients could be overruled anytime doctors or other decision makers believed the patients lacked perfect understanding of their situation. But House's willingness to face felony charges and the possible loss of his medical license makes this an actual case of civil disobedience. If subsequent events work to his disadvantage, House's tenure will not protect him.

Diogenes and Eccentricity

Diogenes of Sinope (404–323 BCE) was the most famous of the Cynics. He distrusted the written word, and if he did write anything, none of it survived. But he was influential enough for others to record his life and views. Diogenes' philosophy stressed living an ethical life, a life as nature intended. Thus, the conventional life of Athens was far too soft, and the polite life of civil society was far too dishonest. Diogenes believed that one's public persona and private persona should be identical—what one says and does in private should be what one says and does in public. Like the later Stoics, he believed material possessions were not conducive to human happiness. In fact, they may well be an impediment. Thus, Diogenes lived simply and without material possessions, flaunting the rules of social convention. It is reported that he defecated and masturbated in public—even House hasn't gone that far . . . yet. Told of Plato's definition of man as a "featherless biped," Diogenes reportedly plucked a chicken and said, "Behold, Plato's man!" Now that does sound like House. Diogenes is perhaps best known for walking the streets during daylight with a lit torch or lantern "looking for an honest man." We are all aware of modern politicians who preach family values in public while privately divorcing their spouses, abandoning their children, or soliciting prostitutes. For Diogenes, if you're going to talk the talk, you'd better walk the walk; only by "walking your talk" can you live ethically and happily.

House exhibits a similar disdain for hypocrisy. Brazenly taking his Vicodin in public, he does nothing to hide his drug use from his colleagues. House routinely tells others exactly what he's thinking and what he's feeling. Of course, conventional morality tells us to be polite, but being polite isn't always honest. And truth is critical to House, who comments on the hypocrisy and dishonesty of his patients and others with his refrain "Everybody lies." Tests must be repeated because tests are unreliable and people make mistakes. Computer-aided testing helps, but occasionally it masks what would be obvious to the human eye. Conventional wisdom is often right, but House is brought in when it is wrong.

Socrates and Eccentricity

Socrates (469–399 BCE) is one of the most eccentric, influential, and important philosophers of all time. Like Diogenes, Socrates distrusted the printed word, and, once again, if he wrote anything, it hasn't survived. Although other contemporaries wrote about Socrates, Socratic scholars believe the most reliable account of his philosophy is found in the dialogues of his most famous student, Plato (427–347 BCE). The earliest of these dialogues is Plato's *Apology*, which purportedly is a transcript of Socrates' testimony at his trial in Athens in 399 BCE. Socrates is found guilty of the crimes of impiety (not worshipping the gods of the state, and inventing other new divinities) and corrupting the youth, and he is sentenced to die by drinking the poison hemlock.

Considering and rejecting exile as a penalty for his "crimes," Socrates states:

Someone will say: Yes, Socrates, but cannot you hold your tongue, and then you may go into a foreign city, and no one will interfere with you? Now I have great difficulty in making you understand my answer to this. For if I tell you that this would be a disobedience to a divine command, and therefore that I cannot hold my tongue, you will not believe that I am serious; and if I say again that the greatest good of man is daily to converse about virtue, and all that concerning which you hear me examining myself and others, and that the life which is unexamined is not worth living—that you are still less likely to believe.[1]

"The unexamined life is not worth living" is certainly one of the most quoted dictums of Socrates and one of the most famous lines in philosophy. Now, exactly what an "examined life" is for Socrates is subject to scholarly debate, but two points are clear enough. One, Socrates is completely unrepentant. Two, Socrates has told the jury he has a definite idea of what a fully human life is, and if he is not to be allowed to live it, then they can go ahead and kill him. If he can't live virtuously, by his own standards of virtue, he would prefer to die.

Socrates' willingness to sacrifice all for the way of life that he thinks is right has won him countless admirers over the centuries. House may well be one of them. While House's actions are routinely insubordinate, outside professional ethics, and even illegal, they often strike us as somewhat noble. House has his own examined way of practicing medicine, and if he is not allowed to do so, he feels that his life would not be worth living.[2]

The Virtue of Eccentricity

So there is something strangely compelling about both House and the eccentrics we find in the history of philosophy. But why? Perhaps eccentrics perform an important service for which we have an intuitive, though largely unarticulated, appreciation. One attempt to flesh out this appreciation is found in the work of John Stuart Mill (1806–1873). Mill, in his own way, is one of the colorful and eccentric figures in the history of philosophy, and *On Liberty*, perhaps his most important work, is a landmark defense of individual liberty. In a part of *On Liberty* that is often overlooked, Mill argues that eccentrics are important to a marketplace of ideas. For Mill there is great public utility in what he calls "Experiments in Living." After all, we will not have a rich debate on the issues of the day if everyone is a product of, and offers a recitation of, the status quo. We would even have a radically diminished debate if relatively few individuals are encouraged to develop their individual capacities. As Mill beautifully states:

> He who lets the world, or his own portion of it, choose his plan of life for him, has no need of any other faculty than the ape-like one of imitation. He who chooses his plan for himself, employs all his faculties. . . . It is possible that he might be guided in some good path, and kept out of harm's way, without any of these things. But what will be his comparative worth as a human being? It really is of importance, not only what men do, but also what manner of men they are that do it. Among the works of man, which human life is rightly employed in perfecting and beautifying, the first in importance surely is man himself. . . . Human nature is not a machine to be built after a model, and set to do exactly the work prescribed for it, but a tree, which requires to grow and develop itself on all sides, according to the tendency of the inward forces which make it a living thing.[3]

House, like the eccentric philosophers we have already examined, is clearly a work in progress. He has not let others choose his plan for him, nor does he engage in the ape-like life of imitation. He is much like Mill's analogy of a tree, growing according to the internal forces that make House, well, House.

Self-development and Moral Progress

Mill is a progressive in the sense that he believes that moral progress is possible. Progress entails change, and significant change requires new thoughts, new attitudes, and new actions. But unless we encourage those who are willing to find their own path, we risk stifling important innovations. He says:

> I insist thus emphatically on the importance of genius, and the necessity of allowing it to unfold itself freely both in thought and in practice, being well aware that no one will deny the position in theory, but knowing also that almost every one, in reality, is totally indifferent to it. . . . Originality is the one thing which unoriginal minds cannot feel the use of. They cannot see what it is to do for them: how should they? If they could see what it would do for them, it would not be originality. The first service which originality has to render them, is that of opening their eyes: which being once fully done, they would have a chance of being themselves original. Meanwhile, recollecting that nothing was ever yet done which some one was not the first to do, and that all good things which exist are the fruits of originality, let them be modest enough to believe that there is something still left for it to accomplish, and assure themselves that they are more in need of originality, the less they are conscious of the want.[4]

Whenever Dr. Cuddy is forced to explain her willingness to deal with House's irregularities, she invariably responds: "He is the best doctor we have." House is the diagnostician of last resort. Patients are referred to House when other doctors are stumped. Those who are unwilling to see the genius in his original approach to diagnostics are, unlike Cuddy, unwilling to put up with his eccentricity.

Eccentricity and Moral Progress

Since Mill is committed to moral progress and the importance of self-development in its creation, he is further committed to the idea that we should encourage others in their originality. But those who stray far from the norm like House and go their own way cross over a fine line. They strike others as not simply original, but rather as outright eccentric. However, Mill thinks this is all to the good:

> In this age the mere example of non-conformity, the mere refusal to bend the knee to custom, is itself a service. Precisely because the tyranny of opinion is such as to make eccentricity a reproach, it is desirable, in order to break through that tyranny, that people should be eccentric. Eccentricity has always abounded when and where strength of character has abounded; and the amount of eccentricity in a society has generally been proportional to the amount of genius, mental vigor, and moral courage which it contained. That so few now dare to be eccentric, marks the chief danger of the time.[5]

House serves the important social function of saving lives when others have no clue. He is an effective teacher and leader of his team. But if Foreman, Cameron, and Chase were not individuals of high character with the requisite amount of "genius, mental vigor, and moral courage," House would not be anywhere near as effective. House needs a team of "characters with character" to function properly (we can hope his new recruits will fit the bill), and only a society willing to let such characters flourish will be able to provide House with his team.

There are obvious costs to being eccentric; after all, others will often find you eccentric! But Mill suggests that our eccentrics perform for us an essential service. They are willing to take on a hostile society in the hope of discovering something meaningful beyond the status quo. As many conservatives are more than willing to tell us, most of these new ideas, opinions, and experiments in life turn out worse than the old ones, and thus, our eccentrics are likely to fail. But this does not mean that they do not provide a useful service. The eccentrics offer their own lives as experiments in living in order to further the goal of creating new role models, new ideas, new opinions, and new experiments in living. Ultimately, they provide the essential service of furthering our search for lives that are truly worth living. But it should be noted that Mill finds a clear connection between the search for a life that is worth living, and a search for the truth. He writes:

> There are, it is alleged, certain beliefs, so useful, not to say indispensable to well-being, that it is as much the duty of governments to uphold those beliefs, as to protect any other of the interests of society. . . . The usefulness of an opinion is itself matter of opinion: as disputable, as open to discussion and requiring discussion as much, as the opinion itself. There is the same need of an infallible judge of opinions to decide an opinion to be noxious, as to decide it to be false, unless the opinion condemned has full opportunity of defending itself. And it will not do to say that the heretic may be allowed to maintain the utility or harmlessness of his opinion, though forbidden to maintain its truth. The truth of an opinion is part of its utility.[6]

The one aspect of House's personality that is most intriguing is his almost seamless ability to connect Mill's search for a life worth living with a search for the truth. In the episode "Occam's Razor," House has this elegant theory that his patient's problems were largely caused by a pharmacist's error. Working under this assumption, he cures the patient. But the pharmacist denies substituting the drug of House's theory for the patient's cough medicine, and the patient and his family cannot rule this out. So House patiently goes through every brand of the drug in the hospital pharmacy until he finds one almost identical to the cough pills. Now one could argue that House's narcissism drives his need to be right, but it also drives his need to know the truth. And in the medical world, the truth of an opinion is clearly part of its utility.

Thus, there is a clear connection between our search for a life worth living and a search for the truth. If the truth of an opinion is part of its utility, and we can find the truth of this opinion only in a free marketplace of ideas, then Mill's moral theory clearly must support a free marketplace of ideas. But a truly vigorous marketplace of ideas—one that is capable of discovering new truths about matters as fundamental as what models we should use to structure our own lives—must let eccentrics and their experiments in living flourish.

As Mill argues in the second and third chapters of *On Liberty*, if we want a society that is capable of a meaningful search for the truth, we want a society in which there is a rich and robust marketplace of ideas. If we want a society in which there is a rich and robust marketplace of ideas, we must encourage eccentrics and their experiments in living. Thus, if we want a society that is capable of a meaningful search for the truth, we must encourage eccentrics and their experiments in living.

House is clearly such an experiment in living, the kind of character described in the country music standard "Mama, Don't Let Your Babies Grow Up to Be Cowboys."

And them that don't know him won't like him.
And them that do sometimes won't know how to take him.
He ain't wrong he's just different

but his pride won't let him do things to make you think he's right.[7]

For many of us, a world that could find no place for House would be a world we would not wish to inhabit. There is much one can learn from the Houses of the world, and there is great social utility in allowing their eccentricity to flourish. Thus we have compelling social reasons to admire eccentrics, and in many cases to treat eccentricity as a virtue.

NOTES

1. Plato, *Apology*. This translation by Benjamin Jowett is available at http://classics.mit.edu/Plato/apology.html.

2. For more on House and the unexamined life, see chapter 1, this volume.

3. John Stuart Mill, *On Liberty* (1859), chapter 3, paragraph 4. Since there are multiple editions of this work in print, I prefer to use chapter and paragraph citations rather than page numbers.

4. Mill, *On Liberty*, chapter 3, paragraph 13.

5. Ibid., chapter 3, paragraph 14.

6. Ibid., chapter 2, paragraph 10.

7. This song, written by Ed and Patsy Bruce, has been performed by such stars as Johnny Paycheck, Waylon Jennings, and most famously by Willie Nelson. Ed Bruce and Patsy Bruce, "Mama, Don't Let Your Babies Grow Up to Be Cowboys" (Memphis: United Artists, 1974). Current copyright: Ed Bruce, Sony/ATV (Tree Publishing Co., Inc., 2007).

LOVE: THE ONLY RISK HOUSE CAN'T TAKE

Sara Protasi

In the first season, Cameron seems to fall in love with her boss. Maybe she is only attracted to him, or maybe she really comes to love him. Determining whether Cameron *truly* loves House is not easy, and you might think that philosophy won't help us. . . . But philosophy defines concepts and the realities that these concepts capture and express, including love. So, with the help of House and philosophy, let's ask: what is love?[1]

The Problem: Why Do You Love Me?

For now, let's assume that Cameron actually loves House. The surly doctor is initially annoyed and resists seduction. Then Cameron blackmails him: either he goes out with her, or she won't come back to work. House surrenders, and they go out on a real date. We can see that he's tempted by the possibility of having a relationship with her. But he ends up repeating to her what he has always believed: that Cameron likes him because she sees him as a lonely, embittered cripple,

198

as someone she could "save" or "fix." Is this such a bad reason for loving someone? House thinks it is. He doesn't want to be loved that way. He doesn't want to feel pitied and loved by virtue of his weakness.

Cameron might reply, though, that House is wrong about her motivation. There can't be reasons for love. She *just* loves him. Love has no reasons, it's irrational! Consequently, there can't be good or bad reasons to love someone, and House is wrong in ridiculing and rejecting her love.

Is Love an Emotion?

Common sense tends to hold that love is an emotion *and* it is irrational: Cupid's arrows strike without reason. But emotions can be either rational or irrational; it can be right or wrong to feel a certain emotion in a given situation. For instance, House's anger is often wrong. Sometimes his anger is disproportionate and sometimes it is just out of place. And sometimes House's anger is also *morally* unjustified; for example, he often gets angry with desperate parents of dying patients. But his anger may nevertheless be appropriate, as it is in "Paternity," when he finds out that his patient's well-intentioned parents didn't tell him the "detail" that the boy had been adopted, which means he might have contracted a virus from his biological mother.

Is love like anger? If Cameron is in love with House because he's an embittered cripple, that doesn't seem to be analogous to the case of a disproportionate or wrongly addressed anger. In the case of anger, the object of the emotion is either appropriate or it isn't: it deserves anger (with that precise intensity) or it doesn't. But love seems to be a different case. It doesn't seem right to describe the object of love as (un)deserving or (in)appropriate. Maybe Cameron is right in denying that her love has any reason. Love cannot be inappropriate just because its object is not lovable (like when we are unjustifiably angry). And we cannot love "too much" (as we are too angry compared to the circumstances). So maybe love isn't an emotion at all.

Love Is a State of the Will

I think Cameron is right about her case, even though in some cases love can be irrational or inappropriate. But love's inappropriateness, its being "right or wrong," is not the same kind of inappropriateness that emotions have. Love is similar to emotions, and to other states of the mind like desires and beliefs, because it is an *intentional* state. In philosophy, this means that love is a (mental) state *about* something. The object that a state is about is called the "intentional object," and in the case of love, it coincides with the object to which love is directed, which is called the "target." This does not happen with every mental state; for instance, I can be angry with someone (target) because she humiliated me (object). Love is not just about the beloved, but also toward the beloved. Love then moves us to action more than other mental states and as much as desires (it is actually very similar to a desire).

Of course, we are also moved *by* love: it is experienced as something that happens to us. This feeling of passivity is explained by the set of emotions that constitute the "feel" of love. The experience of love is characterized not only by physical changes and sensations (like sexual arousal), but also by desires, thoughts, typical behaviors, and of course emotions of various kinds. Since the emotional part of the experience of love is vivid, it is easy to conceive of love as an emotion, even though it isn't.

What is it then? Perhaps love is a state of the will, a volitional state. A volitional state can be a desire (for example, to be with her), a set of desires (for example, to be with her and to make love to her), or a second-order desire, in other words, "a desire about a desire."[2] As an example of a second-order desire, consider when, on balance, I don't want to want a cigarette. I'd like to smoke, but since I know it's bad for my health, I'd also like not to have that desire. Love seems to be a second-order desire. Think about Chase. At the beginning he's simply attracted to Cameron. He likes her and likes having sex with her. But then his desire gets stronger, and he tries hard to convince her to stay with him. His desire isn't something he simply happens to have. He *wants* to have that desire. His love is a "desire about a desire."

Cameron seems to realize that love is a second-order desire. When she realizes that House is still in love with Stacy and that he's not actually incapable of love, she tells him: "You don't want to love *me*." It might seem a strange expression, but it's not. Although love is not voluntary, we do have some control over the context that influences our desires. House is attracted to Cameron, but he chooses not to pursue that attraction. He doesn't come to have a desire for desiring Cameron. So, in some sense, he doesn't want to love Cameron.

Knowledge and Love

House doesn't want to love Cameron because he feels humiliated by her image of him. Stacy, who met House before he was disabled, loves House because he's sexy and brilliant. Cameron probably also finds him sexy and smart, but she sees him primarily as lonely and embittered. House thinks Cameron is not seeing his real self, and he becomes distant. House is right and wrong at the same time. He's right in being suspicious of projections in love. The lover must not be totally ignorant of the beloved's essential qualities. If Cameron loved House thinking that he was a poor, totally defenseless cripple, she would be substantially mistaken about House. She would be loving someone else. House is wrong because he is somewhat as Cameron sees him. She knows House well and loves him as he really is, even though she probably hopes for some change that won't happen.

Properties of the Beloved

Does Cameron love House because he is lonely and embittered, smart and sexy? Is love grounded in the properties of the beloved? It seems that love cannot be based on the qualities of the beloved because we love people throughout life's changes. If someone stops loving his partner because she grows older and less attractive, we say that it's not true love. If a partner gets seriously ill and ceases to be a witty and brilliant person, the other partner will love him anyway, or she will be accused of having superficial feelings.

But someone might respond by distinguishing between two different things: the state of love and the relationship of love. The reasons why a relationship is maintained do not all depend on the person's being in love. Even without assuming particular tragedies, people stay together for many reasons, and the related feelings may evolve through time and, for instance, mutate from erotic passion to esteem and affection. The examples centered on the possibility of loving someone who has been deprived of attractive properties, then, show nothing.

We can also fall out of love as easily as we fall in love, and there may not be particularly good reasons for this change. If I don't love you anymore because you have completely altered your personality, it seems unfair to charge me with untrue love.

We love individuals, not mysterious, amorphous entities. We love a specific person, and persons are constituted by properties.[3] Cameron loves House because he's charming and witty and desperate, even though if asked to say why she loves him, Cameron might just say, "Because House is House."

Still, it is true that we love people who change. Even more true: we love people as they manifest their properties *to us*. House is House, but he relates differently to different people. Cuddy very often sees him as annoying, but less often as abusive, whereas his team might well see him as more often abusive than annoying. Because they see his fragility more clearly, Wilson and Cuddy try to protect him more than Chase or Foreman do. Stacy, who was in love with House, knows some of his qualities that no one else knows or has experienced. So a good property theory should account for these features and claim that we love in virtue of properties that change both in time and as a consequence of a relationship. Unlike height or date of birth, which are characteristics of House that are fixed for everyone and in every time, being annoying and abusive are relative. And the same is true for his charm and his wit.

Okay, so Cameron loves House because he's charming, witty, and desperate. But at the end of the third season she ends up loving Chase, who is somehow the opposite of House. He's conformist, sweet (with her, at least), and not desperate at all. Cameron loves Chase, and not someone else, because he's such and such. So why did she love House but now Chase?

Love Is Creative

Why does Cameron stop loving House even if he has the same properties, and begin to love Chase, who has a totally different set of properties? Part of the answer is that love is a second-order desire. It is the commitment to a liking. So, as much as it comes, it also goes away. The qualities that characterize the beloved are essential only for the liking, for the first-order desire, but they do not determine the second-order volition. Cameron is attracted to House because he has certain characteristics. Then, in virtue of her having a second-order desire (which may be influenced by the fact she needs to give love to needy and desperate people, for instance), she falls in love with him. House thus acquires for her an incommensurable *value*, which does not depend on his qualities anymore. That value, that importance, is *created* by the love itself. This is why when we love, we attribute value to our beloved's interests, pursuits we didn't care about before that person came into our lives. But when House does not reciprocate her love, and denies he needs her help, she realizes that she can love someone else who is capable of accepting her help, like Chase. She therefore withdraws from him and from her desire for him. And with the end of the love comes the loss of value that was created by it. This is why, even though people remain the same, love can end or even turn to hate.

Is Erotic Love Moral?

The contemporary philosopher Harry Frankfurt claims that love (in general) is a particular second-order volition: a disinterested concern for the beloved's well-being. According to this definition, Cameron seems to be truly in love with House. So is she an altruistic sweet young woman who just desires House's happiness even though he doesn't treat her with respect and kindness?

Cameron *is* a sweet and morally irreproachable woman. I doubt, though, that her erotic love for House is such. After all, when it comes to seducing House, she fights hard, even blackmailing him (yes, it's a sweet blackmail, but it's still blackmail). *Eros* seems to turn even the mild Cameron into a bolder person, and this metamorphosis becomes evident in her audacious and self-assured proposal to Chase in the third season (although the attitude toward Chase is not driven by love, at least at the beginning). This is not to deny that love is ever moral, but only to say that it is not necessarily so. There are many ways of manifesting and living erotic love, maybe as many as the number of lovers. Still, they have something in common: the fact of being in love, of course. But what is the content of the loving desire? What does Cameron want from House?

The answer does not seem to be sex, even though sexuality is often a part of the experience of *eros*. Cameron is probably physically attracted by the troubled charm of her boss, but it doesn't seem to be at the core of her love. She doesn't just want to sleep with him. She also wants to hug him, be part of his life, feel desired by him, share time and activities with him, and so on. She wants to be his other half. She is not being altruistic. She wants something for herself. She wants to be complete. This is the real nature of erotic desire: matching with a person.[4]

House behaves immorally with Stacy, spying on her confidences to her psychoanalyst and trying to sabotage her marriage. He's a real jackass on more than one occasion, and still no viewer would deny that he loves her. He knows her well, he desires her physically, and he wants to stay with her. We don't need much more to claim he's in love with Stacy.

You might object that House's love for Stacy *is* moral. After all, isn't it out of consideration for her that he ends the relationship? Yes, but I don't think he does it out of *eros*. Rather, he does it because he feels affection for Stacy and because even House is sometimes capable of moral actions. He does it because he thinks it's the right thing to do, as when he thinks a leg has to be amputated. Recall that he also does the right thing with Cameron. He keeps her distant as much as he can, until he's forced to go out with her. And therefore he's sensitive to other people's requests not to hurt her.

But *eros* in itself is not moral. Cameron might disagree. But she didn't think about ethics when she forced House to go out with her. In fact, she was so proud of it that she didn't even hide their agreement, as House asked her to do. Because of *eros*, and not because of mere sexual attraction, people are prone to commit every kind of act. As C. S. Lewis convincingly puts it: "The love which leads to cruel and perjured unions, even to suicide pacts and murder, is not likely to be wandering lust or idle sentiment. It may well be Eros in all his splendour; heart-breakingly sincere; ready for every sacrifice except renunciation."[5]

Why House Can't Love:
Vulnerability in Love

But the analysis of the "House-Cameron" case is not yet complete. We have seen Cameron's reasons, but not House's. Why does he ultimately reject Cameron? We suspect that he has been partially insincere in presenting his case against having the relationship. He is certainly irritated by Cameron's pitiful love. But in his self-pitying and yet contradictorily self-confident consideration of his capacities and skills, he must realize that if he weren't the blue-eyed, witty, charming, brilliant scientist that he is, she would probably devote her loving capacity to someone else. As we have seen, erotic love is directed toward specific individuals, with a set of characteristic properties. When House, for a short period, regains the use of his leg muscle, he invites Cameron to go out, but she doesn't seem interested. He claims that she is not interested anymore because he's healthy now and has changed. Cameron, correctly, remarks that he hasn't changed much. The pain, however, will come back, and House will use his cane again. But House is right too in noticing a change of attitude in Cameron. Whatever the reason might be, she is not in love with him anymore. Love is not eternal; even genuine love can end.

And this is very scary. This is why fairy tales ending with "They lived happily ever after" are so appealing. This is also why we're moved by tragic stories like that of Romeo and Juliet. Their love will last forever because they won't have the time to grow old and tired of each other (at least, so House would cynically observe). We'd like true love to be eternal. If there were such a thing, maybe we could be lucky enough to find it. Love needs a lot of work, and House is very aware of this. He often does not believe his patients' declarations of love (and fidelity), and he's often right. He is not even convinced by the Cuban Esteban, who risks his life to cure his wife's mysterious illness. House is too much aware of love's failures.

Being naïve is bad, but being cynical is even worse. It prevents House from being happy in many ways, for instance, by leading him to reject the love of a beautiful, intelligent woman.

Wilson often tells House that he wants to be unhappy, and this is why he keeps people away. But Wilson more than anyone else knows the reason why House prefers solitude: because he's too fragile and incapable of accepting the risk involved in human relationships in general, and erotic love in particular. This is why he warns both Cameron and Stacy not to hurt him. They're both surprised, and actually everyone perceives each of them as the weak counterpart. But they will end up being, respectively, with Chase and Mark. They are able to love, to get hurt, to run risks, to begin a new story, to put the pieces back together. House is not. He'll end up alone again.

Love of every kind involves a capacity to trust, an openness to being hurt, and a vulnerability to the other person. This is why House has problems not only in loving a woman, but also in having friends. Even with Wilson, his only friend, he is constantly defensive. Their friendship is based only on Wilson's ability to keep it alive, on his capacity for forgiving House and being patient. Certainly House is attached to Wilson, but he does whatever he can to dominate him. This can work in a friendly relationship, which is less tight and exclusive than a romantic one. But his struggle for being in control of everything cannot work within the context of *eros*, where a peculiar sort of trusting intimacy is fundamental.

By staying away, House has behaved morally with Cameron and above all with Stacy, knowing that he would make them suffer. But the reason he's unable to make them happy is that he's too afraid of the possibility of getting hurt. Unfortunately, that possibility lies at the core of every love experience.

NOTES

1. In this chapter we'll be concerned with romantic love, what the Greeks called *eros*. This is as opposed to love of friends (*philia*), love of intimate relatives (*storge*), and love

of God (*agape*). For an exposition of these distinctions (from a Christian point of view), see C. S. Lewis, *The Four Loves* (San Diego: Harcourt, 1991).

2. Many authors consider love a volitional state, rather than an emotion, among them Robert Nozick and Harry Frankfurt. See Robert Nozick, "Love's Bond," in his book *The Examined Life: Philosophical Meditations* (New York: Simon and Schuster, 1989); and Harry Frankfurt, *Reasons of Love* (Princeton: Princeton Univ. Press, 2004).

3. It might be hard to specify which properties are the ones in virtue of which I love you, but the fact that a theory is hard to test doesn't mean it's wrong. Put in (slightly different) philosophical terms: the question concerning the knowledge we can have of a certain reality is different from the question about the nature and functioning of that reality. The first is an *epistemological* question (*episteme* means "knowledge" in ancient Greek), the second an *ontological* one (from *ontos*, that is, "being").

4. This is a story told by the dramatist Aristophanes in a Platonic dialogue, the Symposium. Plato is one of the most important philosophers of all time, and he lived in Athens between the fifth and fourth centuries BCE. Aristophanes was his contemporary, and in this fictional dialogue Plato imagines him telling a story about the origin of the sexes and of sexual desire and reproduction. The story is complicated and fascinating, and aims to explain not just heterosexual, but also homosexual, attraction. The main idea is that human beings used to be round, and that they have been cut into two parts that now crave each other.

5. See Lewis, *The Four Loves*, 108.

A PRESCRIPTION FOR FRIENDSHIP

Sara Waller

House's patients and colleagues routinely feel used, dismissed, and indelicately handled. Yet Cameron, Wilson, Foreman, and Cuddy frequently stand up for him, lie for him, and save his job. Are they true friends with one another, or are House's colleagues simply masochists? Consider this conversation between Wilson and a patient:

> Patient: He's your friend huh?
>
> Wilson: Yeah.
>
> Patient: Does he care about you?
>
> Wilson: I think so.
>
> Patient: You don't know?
>
> Wilson: As Dr. House likes to say, "Everybody lies."

Patient: It's not what people say, it's what they do.

Wilson: Yeah, he cares about me.

Is Wilson deluded? Is he just another all-too-caring doctor who desperately searches for the good in people, even a colleague as crusty and unmanageable as House, ultimately making himself an enabler to a drug addict? Actually, I think that Wilson is correct in his assertion that he and House are friends. Beyond that, they're not just friends in some trivial sense. According to Aristotle (384–322 BCE), some friendships are based on utility, others on pleasure, and yet others on virtue. The friendship between House and Wilson is not based on utility—it's not just about what they can do for one another. Their friendship is also not based on pleasure. This is not to say that there is no utility or pleasure involved in their relationship. It's just that the relationship is ultimately based on something more meaningful, virtue. And, as we shall see, the same goes for other friendships on the show.

What Does It Take to Be a Friend?

For Aristotle, perfect friendship (meaning friendship in the sense of *haplos*, or without limitation or pollution) is "the friendship of men who are good, and alike in virtue . . . now those who wish well to their friends for their sake are most truly friends."[1] Let's consider what Aristotle means by "good" in this statement. First, friendship is between good people, not just any people. Aristotle is suggesting that there is no friendship among the truly corrupt. You cannot be evil and have evil friends. Good people can have friends because they can truly wish each other well *for their own sake*, that is, without self-interest or hidden agendas. Second, Aristotle is suggesting that people who are good are not just morally good—they are also good at something. For Aristotle, to be good means fulfilling one's function well. Being morally virtuous is not enough—you must also have skill, ability, or talent, and you must be thoughtful—you must have intellectual virtue as well as moral virtue. To "do the good" is to fulfill one's function. For example, "the good" for a diagnostician is not just to solve the case (though that is good for the hospital, the patient, and the careers of the doctor) but to treat the patients. The doctor must do the right thing for the right reason.

Aristotle uses the Greek word *arête*, which means *excellence*, to talk about the defining feature of a truly good individual, capable of the highest form of friendship. Having *arête* means being well-rounded—one must be good morally, intellectually, and socially. According to Aristotle the best life is lived in society, fulfilling the duties of a good citizen.

This is a pretty tall order. The flaws and foibles of the characters make the show continually interesting. House is sarcastic and irreverent, bending and breaking rules whenever he can. Wilson comes across as too caring, and he misleads the women he marries into believing he will always have time for them. Cameron is so emotionally involved with her patients that she cannot tell them bad news. Chase is occasionally so careerist that he makes deals with House's superiors to preserve his own position. And Foreman is not above stabbing Cameron with a needle, thus exposing her to an unknown infectious disease (not to mention stealing her article). Yet, despite their flaws, Cameron, Wilson, Chase, Foreman, and House all at least strive toward some form of *arête*.

Are House and Wilson Really Friends? (or "Everything Sucks, So You Might as Well Find Something to Smile About")

The stage for friendship is set, and the importance of fulfilling one's function is spotlighted, right from the start of the first episode of the first season. Wilson lies to House about his relationship to a patient, claiming that she is his cousin, to get House interested in working on the case. In House's words, Wilson lied to a friend to save a stranger. Why? Because House's function in society is to be a doctor in the hospital. The larger purpose of his life is to heal (not just to solve cases, as he thinks), and he is not going to do it without extra encouragement. Wilson reminds him that his team is doing nothing, and that their purpose is to solve cases: "What is the point of putting together a team if you are not going to use them? You've got three overqualified doctors working for you, getting bored." So begins a wonderful journey of friendship—Aristotle's mutual well-wishing *haplos*. There will be lies, manipulations, and genuine affection in persuading a true friend to fulfill his capabilities and his obligations in the context of a larger social institution—the hospital. The personality trait that makes House unlikely to achieve *arête* and thus fail to fulfill his function and achieve happiness is exactly his propensity to limit himself to puzzle-solving rather than embracing the multifaceted spectrum of life as a diagnostician—with human relationships as well as intellectual stimulation. Wilson continually pushes him to do better, be broader, and embrace more.

In order to push each other toward excellence, House and Wilson must be equal in goodness: talent and virtue. House and Wilson are both good at something. They are both department heads at Princeton-Plainsboro Hospital; House is a legendary diagnostician, Wilson is a well-rounded oncologist. They both have talents beyond mere medicine that help them fulfill their hospital functions with excellence. House can head a team of three doctors without missing a beat. Wilson's gift is the ability to tell patients they have but a few months to live and have them thank him for it. House can manipulate the organ transplant committee with ease, and he usually finds a way to get what he wants in spite of Cuddy's efforts. Wilson has an even temper and great insight into the workings of human emotions, including those of House. The friends are equal in abilities and talents, as well as in social status.

Are they equally good in terms of virtue? One might think that House is the scoundrel while Wilson is the kind, long-suffering friend who bails House out of jail and tolerates his constant abuse. But Wilson is not so virtuous. Wilson has, after all, been "lying to him in increasing increments since he told House that his haircut looked nice last year," and he has continually conspired with Cuddy to deceive and manipulate House in a variety of ways ranging from taking cases (Wilson lies in the first episode about his cousin), to where he moved after his divorce (into the apartment of a patient-lover), to the effectiveness of House's patient care. (Wilson encourages Cuddy to deceive House about the effectiveness of a cortisol shot in a patient with Addison's disease. The patient was cured, but Wilson was concerned that if House understood the accuracy of his diagnosis, he might become even more arrogant, and his "wings might melt.") At the outset of season three, Wilson and Cuddy review files and suggest methods of presentation that will best manipulate House into taking a case. Everybody lies? At the very least, these two best friends lie to each other regularly. They are, after all, alike in virtue.

We might think that a friendship in which two people lie to each other must be anything but perfect. But the mutual deceit shows that one is not more virtuous than the other. They both have foibles. Wilson sleeps with a patient and emotionally abandons his wives. House is so tactless that he costs the hospital more in legal expenses than any other doctor. We see each secretly slipping the other potent drugs (Wilson slips House antidepressants, House slips Wilson amphetamines). And yet, when Wilson's marriage collapses, House opens his door and his home (if only to delight in stealing Wilson's food and tricking him into doing dishes). When House is about to be fired by Vogler, Wilson votes for his friend, risking his position on the board. In seasons one and two, their friendship unfolds in a way that shows two men who are alike in virtue, who are bonded to each other, and who support each other when the chips are down.

Because they both have flaws, neither is perfectly excellent. But Aristotle cautions us to "call no man happy until he is dead." That is, the happiness that comes with a good life, that comes with *arête*, that comes with fulfilling one's function, cannot be complete until a life is finished. We all have things we strive toward in life, because we all have flaws. The fulfillment is in the striving toward perfection. And lies are useful in that they help the two friends improve in other ways. Wilson manipulates patients because his social talent makes him a better doctor overall. House abuses his team because it helps him reach correct diagnoses. Wilson lies to get House to take cases and heal patients. House torments Wilson by eating his food, showing him that in the darkness of divorce, life can still be full of pranks and tomfoolery. House and Wilson show us how we can use our weaknesses to build our strengths, to strive toward excellence—excellence in fulfilling their function as doctors in the social context of the hospital.

The Vogler Challenge

Vogler, who has given the hospital $100 million in exchange for being chairman of the board, takes an immediate dislike to House. First, Vogler wants House to wear a lab coat—a demand he at first resists. Then Vogler wants House to fire a member of his team. When House offers to put into effect Cameron's proposed compromise of cutting everyone's pay to reduce the overall budget of the diagnostic unit, Vogler says no. His concern is not money or efficiency, but control. Vogler then offers House a way out: if he gives a speech touting Vogler's company's new drug, House can keep his team. Cuddy and Wilson are both relieved—showing that they initially value House's cooperation, and Vogler's money, more than House's pride or principled refusal to be controlled. If House gives the speech, he can save the jobs of his team, and since the drug actually works, they view the speech as an acceptable compromise. Cuddy and

Wilson agree that compromise is the best option, contributing to the function of the hospital, the best performance of all doctors involved, and the ultimate well-being of the patients.

House sees things differently. He gives a poor, offensive speech, thus rejecting the deal. Why? Because while he agrees that the ultimate purpose of a hospital is healing, he believes that in order to perform that function, doctors need to be able to make free choices. That is, a hospital is not a business. Choices that make profits are not necessarily in the patients' best interests, or in the interests of the progress of medicine. The great evil here is neither the promotion of the drug nor the trade for his staff, but compromises that limit medical freedom and the choices of medical professionals made in support of their patients. While Wilson and Cuddy disagree with House regarding the best course of action in this case, they agree that the good of the hospital must be served. They are friends because they are ultimately having a rational discourse about the right thing to do. As Cameron says upon quitting, she at first believed that House did everything he did because it would help people, but now she knows that he does everything he does because it is right. The function of the hospital is higher than simply helping people. A hospital heals, supports patients, promotes medical research, and affords doctors with choices. For Cameron and House, what is right is defined not just by success in patient treatment, but by guarding the future of medicine and medical practice.

Despite their disagreement over the right action in this case, Wilson, as a member of the board, votes to keep House. Vogler responds by having Wilson voted off the board. When House confronts him, Wilson says, "I voted to keep you, . . . I only had two things that worked for me: this job and this stupid screwed-up friendship. Neither mattered enough to you to give one lousy speech." Wilson feels abandoned, and he questions the quality of the friendship. House answers: "They mattered."

But they both agree that House would have done the same thing if he had to do it all over again. House does not want to sacrifice Wilson or lose Vogler's donation. But he can't let himself compromise his own (and in consequence, others') freedom to diagnose and treat patients as they see fit. So if we are to worry about mutual well-wishing without interference from one's own projects or ego drives, what House wants is something he wants for everyone. The freedom to make medical decisions is in Wilson's interests so long as Wilson continues to function as a doctor. House is actually, if perhaps irritatingly, working to make sure that Wilson's job does continue to work for him—that if he is a doctor, he can make the choices he needs to make in the best interests of treating patients. And that is being a true friend, for it is an action that promotes Wilson's well-being, even though House is convinced that he too will be fired from his tenured position in short order. Wilson could not be happy if he continued to work at the hospital while unable to make choices. And Wilson would be unable to respect House if House did not stand up for his principles and act on what he thought was right.

The Tritter Challenge

When House is arrested by Tritter in season three, Tritter pressures Wilson to testify by revoking his prescription privileges and freezing his bank account. At first, Wilson suffers and House does nothing to fix the problem. When Wilson needs Cameron to prescribe for him, House refuses to let her assist Wilson. Wilson is furious (and rightly so, on an Aristotelian model of friendship, because here, House is genuinely interfering with Wilson's excellence as a medical professional and social function as a doctor). In "Finding Judas" Wilson watches Cuddy burst into tears after an unkind remark from House about her mothering abilities, sees Chase get a bruised chin, and observes the team members as they endure police questioning and have their assets frozen. House is blocking everyone's excellence and everyone's happiness by refusing to admit that he treated Tritter wrongly, and that he has a serious Vicodin addiction.

Wilson finally tells Tritter he will testify. On the surface, it looks like Wilson may have betrayed House when the going got tough, but ultimately Wilson decided to interfere with House's excellence and social function only after House failed to maintain the friendship and compromised his own excellence in the process. Though Wilson chides House in an earlier episode, saying that his enabling "is not something you should be complaining about," Wilson is not an enabler. He takes a stand, encourages House to go to rehab, and does not back down until House convincingly apologizes and has made several steps (false though they turned out to be) down the road to recovery.

Later, and after House has apologized to him, Wilson refuses to testify against him, because ultimately House fulfills his function at the hospital, and saves lives, more than Wilson does. Even though Tritter promises to charge Wilson with interfering with an investigation, Wilson accepts—better for the patients if he goes to jail than House. Cuddy seems to agree with Wilson by her testimony in "Words and Deeds" as she frees House by perjuring herself. The case is dismissed, but Cuddy is again unconvinced that she did the right thing by preserving House's ability to fulfill his function as a doctor. She recalls the recent events in which House was a hindrance to the rest of the hospital staff, and she offers harsh words: "You make everyone around you worse for being there. The only bright spot is now I own your ass." As an administrator, she is charged with making the hospital manifest *arête*. She saved House because she believes his presence makes the hospital better (or at least that he has the potential to do so). Perhaps Cuddy believes she can use her newfound power to make House fulfill his function and contribute to the excellence of the hospital. And she is willing to make him feel guilty in order to achieve that end.

Such manipulation is worthy of House himself! His only notion of helping people fulfill their function is to make them feel bad. He constantly rides his team in order to "make their self-esteem hinge on the job." While Wilson and Cuddy often disagree with his methods, insisting that guilt and ego invest-ment are not the only way to mold excellent doctors, House might note that it does work, and thus, it is good. Similarly, House believes that he must be on heavy doses of painkillers in order to achieve excellence. Cuddy and Wilson disagree, hoping for a better, brighter, less addicted life for House that would contribute to his overall excellence.

Chase and Cameron:
Does Sex Ruin Friendships?

The sexual tension between Chase and Cameron begins in epi-sode three of season one. In the context of a conversation about the relative safety of a patient's sexual activities, Cameron sug-gests that sex could be dangerous, and Chase asks Cameron if she had ever taken a life during intercourse. Foreman then suggests to Cameron that she has gained power over Chase by discussing sex so boldly.

The sexual tension deepens when Cameron, high on crystal meth, Ecstasy, or both, seduces a rather surprised Chase. They decide not to do it again, agreeing that continued sexual rela-tions would interfere with their *arête* and their ability to function in the workplace. When they begin a "friends-with-benefits" relationship again in season three, it is for the same reasons. That is, life would be more fun and more fulfilling with a con-venient sexual partner than without. A bewildered Chase likens the relationship to microwave pizza, but Cameron reasons, since they did not get "weird" about it the first time ("Of all the people I work with, you're the one I'm least likely to fall in love with"), then there is no reason to believe that a convenient sexual relationship will not improve their functioning through increased physical fulfillment. They take the time to make an agreement that the relationship will not harm either party, that their professional lives will continue unimpeded. Mutual well-wishing is apparent, as well as a bit of lust.

Of course, the agreement does not work out well. Chase wants more, and Cameron rebuffs him (at first). And, as Foreman has been warning, it affects the entire team's ability to function: "Oh crap, you two are agreeing again." When they are sleeping together, they agree on diagnoses and treatment plans and leave a patient in a sleep disorder diagnostics room alone (only to panic and be saved by Foreman). When they are not sleeping together, they argue and bicker and compete for House's approval. They don't stop wishing each other well in any deeper sense—neither of them quits or tries to get the other fired, neither intentionally interferes with the other's medical practice. They continue to wish each other well; they just don't want to be in close quarters with one another until the emotional situation settles down (and House takes great glee in assigning them to break into a home together, run tests together, and so on). Chase and Cameron were friends who simply bit off more than they could chew. They still treat each other as equals, as professionals, but their emotional situation interferes with both their excellence and their happiness (and that of others) by impairing their ability to function with each other as team members. Maybe lovers can be friends, but these two decreased their excellence as they increased their physical contact.

Cameron and Foreman
Aren't Friends—or Are They?

"Look, Cameron is a friend," says Foreman to House in season one as House prepares to take her on a date—Cameron's condition for returning to work after the Vogler challenge.

Foreman has decided to protect Cameron, to assist in preserving her well-being by making sure she is not romantically harmed by the gruff and unsympathetic House. Foreman most clearly seems to value the functioning of the team. He repeatedly says that he chose to work with House to learn from him (and perhaps he has learned too much by the end of season three), in other words, to perfect his own excellence as a doctor. Of course it is in Foreman's interests to make sure the team functions smoothly, but he had many options upon approaching House before the date. He could have urged House not to go, or to offer her another condition for reemployment. Instead, he claims Cameron as a friend worthy of protection—an equal, a person with feelings, a person who wishes him well in return.

So it is surprising that upon being confronted for stealing Cameron's notes, Foreman responds by telling her, "We're not friends, we're colleagues." Foreman allows self-interest to override his well-wishing for Cameron, adding insult to injury by potentially infecting her after he has contracted a mysterious and potentially fatal illness in "Euphoria." Indeed, he actually wishes her ill in order to facilitate his own diagnosis. Cameron returns the sentiment in kind, accepting his request for her to be his medical proxy (revealing that he did read her article, and that he does respect her opinion and scholarship), but rejecting his apology and bid for her forgiveness and friendship. That is, she is willing to fulfill her function in a way that promotes her own well-being, just as Foreman did. But she is not willing to allow Foreman to call them friends. When he finally apologizes, she accepts, but it takes time for the relationship to heal.

This is a case of a friendship gone wrong due to egocentric aims. Neither works well with the other when Foreman puts a publishing credit ahead of their friendship, and Cameron responds with her own career concerns by talking with Cuddy about the situation. When they say goodbye at the end of season three, Cameron gives Foreman a framed memento of their falling-out, perhaps needling him a bit about his theft. Will they be friends in ten years or will they just send each other Christmas cards? The answer lies in their ability to place mutual well-wishing above their careerism and their egos.

Pursuing Excellence

Whether the challenge is Vogler, Tritter, sexual attraction, or careerism, the free and equal exchange of ideas among friends and colleagues is the glue that holds the team together. What tears them apart at the end of season three is only the desire for continued excellence. Foreman sees that being an excellent doctor is not identical to being House, Chase sees that pursuit of keeping his job at the expense of his integrity and self-respect is not worthwhile, and Cameron sees that House does not always do what is right. Though they pursue what they think is good in different and conflicting ways, we can hope that these friends will continue to advocate for *arête* and will continue to wish one another well.

NOTES

1. Aristotle, *The Basic Works of Aristotle, Nicomachean Ethics*, ed. and trans. Richard McKeon (New York Random House), 1941), Book 8, Chapter 3, 1156b.

DIAGNOSING CHARACTER: A HOUSE DIVIDED?

Heather Battaly and Amy Coplan

Rebecca [patient]: Is [Dr. House] a good man?

Wilson: He's a good doctor.

Rebecca: Can you be one without the other? Don't you have to care about people?

Wilson: Caring is a good motivator; he's found something else.

—"Pilot"

Foreman [to House]: In order to be like you as a doctor, I have to be like you as a human being. I don't want to turn into you.

— "Family"

How can Gregory House be such a terrific doctor and such a terrible person at the same time? Is Rebecca, the patient in the pilot episode, correct? Must one be a good person to be a good doctor? Foreman doesn't seem to think so. In fact, in "Family," he claims that in order to be a diagnostician of House's caliber, one cannot be a good person—rather, one must be the kind of person House is. We think that Foreman is correct. House's impaired character doesn't interfere with his being an outstanding doctor; on the contrary, it is required for it. Being a better person morally would make House a worse diagnostician.

Patient Gregory House

House is clearly a skilled diagnostician, reliably generating true beliefs about the illnesses of his patients.[1] House uses the skill of fine-grained perception to pick up on cues that others overlook. He notices involuntary muscle spasms, faked reactions to pain, and tiny anomalies on MRI films. House uses the inductive skill of inference to the best explanation in almost every episode—he finds the simplest explanation for all of the patient's symptoms. House also uses the skills of deductive reasoning. For instance, he routinely reasons as follows: If the patient had cancer, then it would either show up on an MRI or in blood tests. It did not show up on an MRI or in blood tests, so the patient does not have cancer.

Do these diagnostic skills make House a good person morally? Definitely not. To be a good person morally, one must possess the moral virtues, character traits including benevolence, justice, courage, and temperance, to name a few. One can be skilled in multiple ways—diagnostically, musically, athletically—without being morally virtuous. Master thieves, for example, are adept at stealing, but they are not just. While skills, like stealing, can be used for bad ends, moral virtues cannot.

Do House's diagnostic skills make him a good person intellectually? After all, he is an outstanding diagnostician—he reliably arrives at true beliefs about the illnesses of his patients. But these skills alone are not enough. To be a good person intellectually, one must possess the intellectual virtues, character traits including open-mindedness, care in gathering and evaluating evidence, intellectual courage, and intellectual autonomy. And to possess those virtues, one must care about the truth for its own sake, not for some ulterior end like money or fame. One can be skilled at induction, deduction, and diagnosis without caring about the truth for its own sake. For instance, students in a logic class might become skilled at deduction and induction not because they value the truth for its own sake but because they want good grades. Even skilled diagnosticians might be ultimately motivated by money or reputation—they might not care about truth for its own sake (though this does not describe House). If one doesn't care about truth for its own sake, then however adept one may be at attaining true beliefs, one is not intellectually virtuous. So does House have the intellectual virtues?

On the Blackboard:
What Are the Virtues?

Our definition of virtue is based on Aristotle's (384–322 BCE) theory of the moral virtues.[2] Virtues are habits of appropriate action, emotion, choice, perception, and motivation. To be virtuous, one must perform virtuous actions. For example, the open-minded person listens to others when it is appropriate to do so; those who do not are not open-minded. The benevolent person helps others when it is appropriate to do so; those who do not are not benevolent. To be virtuous one must also be appropriately motivated. Simply doing what the virtuous person would do does not make one virtuous. Helping others when it is appropriate to do so is not enough for benevolence, and listening to others when it is appropriate to do so is not enough for open-mindedness. One must also do those acts for the right reasons. Manipulators, for example, help and listen to others, but are motivated by personal gain rather than by caring about others or the truth.

The characters on *House* sometimes do what virtuous people would do. (This does not necessarily mean that they have fully acquired the virtues.) To illustrate, in "Histories," Foreman and Wilson care about their patient, Victoria, and do not want her to die alone. They leave the hospital in search of James, a person Victoria mentions. Even though they do not find James, they try to. (Unfortunately, they discover that James, Victoria's son, was killed in an accident.) They do what a benevolent person would do in these circumstances. In "Paternity," Chase tackles a patient who is hallucinating to prevent him from walking off the roof of the hospital. Here, Chase does what the courageous person would do.

House repeatedly listens to alternative diagnoses offered by his team, and by Wilson and Cuddy. He repeatedly does what the open-minded person would do. In "Love Hurts," Foreman initially suggests that the patient, Harvey, has bacterial endo-carditis (an infection of the heart valve). Chase suggests that Harvey has an aneurysm as a result of trauma. The team then acquires new evidence: they see Harvey's "friend" Annette choking him, and determine that she is a dominatrix. Foreman admits that given this new evidence, Chase's diagnosis is more likely to be correct than his own. In this situation, Foreman does what the intellectually courageous person would do—he retracts his initial diagnosis.

House Lacks Moral Virtue

House is a spectacular misanthrope who repeatedly fails to do what a benevolent person would do. He is unnecessarily cruel to patients and their families, and to his colleagues and friends.

He routinely issues gratuitous insults and is so consistently callous that we are shocked on the rare occasion when he manages to show compassion. Since House repeatedly fails to do what a benevolent person would do, he is not benevolent.

House also repeatedly violates his patients' and colleagues' rights to privacy. To illustrate, in "Paternity," House runs DNA tests on the coffee cups of his patient's parents without their consent in order to win a bet that they are not the genetic parents of his patient. He also reads Wilson's, Cameron's, and Stacy's private medical files without their consent. Since he repeatedly fails to do what the just person would do, House is not just.

Though House cares about finding the truth, he does not care about telling the truth. He lies to Tritter, and he lies to his colleagues about being off Vicodin. He also deceives other doctors. For example, in "The Socratic Method," he intentionally tricks a surgeon into operating on his patient—he shrinks the patient's tumor so that it is small enough to be removed by the surgeon. Since he repeatedly fails to do what the honest person would do, House is not honest.

House lacks some of the moral virtues—nothing shocking there. It would be considerably more shocking, however, if we found House lacking in intellectual virtue. He certainly appears to have intellectually virtuous motivations—after all, he cares about finding the truth (solving the puzzle) for its own sake; he does not care about truth primarily as a means to some other end like wealth, fame, or even the health of his patients. House also appears to regularly perform intellectually virtuous actions—he considers alternative hypotheses, defends his diagnoses against objections, and gathers evidence from tests, medical journals, and patients' homes. House seems to be a downright paragon of intellectual virtue. Yet some of these appearances may be deceiving. Philosophers such as Plato and Aristotle argue that one either has all of the virtues, or none of them. This is called the Unity of the Virtues Thesis. And it would imply that since House obviously doesn't have all the virtues, he has no virtues.

The Unity of the Virtues

In this view, House's character illness is systemic. All of House's character traits, moral and intellectual, are infected because all of those traits are interconnected. Life is messy. A single situation can raise issues relevant to more than one virtue. For example, imagine that Cuddy has come to care deeply about a patient in kidney failure. Should she use her power to move that patient to the top of the transplant list even though there is no medical reason for doing so? Cuddy must simultaneously be appropriately sensitive to considerations of benevolence and justice—she must recognize that although she wants to help this patient, moving her to the top of the list would be unfair to patients already on that list. The virtues of benevolence and justice intersect, and if Cuddy isn't appropriately responsive to others' rights, she will be neither just nor benevolent. There is nothing special about benevolence and justice in this regard. Each moral virtue will intersect with every other moral virtue. Life is complicated, and issues overlap. In short, if one is not appropriately responsive to concerns about others' rights, this will not only prevent one from being just, but also from being benevolent, temperate, and courageous, too. Since each moral character trait intersects with all of the others, one infected trait will contaminate them all.

The same can be said of the intellectual virtues. To illustrate, in "Damned If You Do," Cameron diagnoses the patient as having an allergic reaction. One of Cameron's colleagues thinks that she is wrong—that the patient isn't having an allergic reaction, and that instead she has an autoimmune disease. Should Cameron consider this alternative diagnosis, or should she stand up for her own belief? Should she second-guess herself? That all depends on the context: which colleague posed the diagnosis and his area of expertise, whether Cameron knows more than he does about this area, how sure she is of her own diagnosis, whether she already used reasonable evidence to eliminate autoimmune diseases, and so on. To be open-minded one must avoid excess naïveté: avoid considering alternatives one shouldn't. But sometimes avoiding naïveté requires defending your own beliefs—being appropriately sensitive to the concerns of intellectual courage.

At the end of the same episode, House berates Cameron for failing to stand up for her diagnosis. Let's assume that House is correct and that Cameron has been an intellectual coward. If so, she has simultaneously been naïve. This demonstrates that the virtue of open-mindedness intersects with the virtue of intellectual courage. There is nothing special about open-mindedness and intellectual courage in this regard. We can expect each intellectual virtue to intersect with every other intellectual virtue. If one is not appropriately responsive to concerns about defending one's beliefs, one will not only fail to be intellectually courageous, but also fail to be open-minded, intellectually autonomous, and careful about gathering evidence, too. In sum, if one intellectual character trait is off-target, all of them will be off-target, since they are all interconnected.

Finally, and most important, life is so messy that our moral and intellectual lives also intersect. Examples abound. Consider a routine case in which the concerns of justice intersect with the concerns of caring about gathering evidence. Suppose that you have two young children—unfortunately, one is a troublemaker and the other is a manipulator. One of them is responsible for breaking a valuable heirloom, but you don't know which child did it. Each blames the other. If you don't care enough about the truth and thus don't gather further evidence, then your decision to punish only one or the other child will be unjust. It's not only justice and caring about evidence that intersect; each moral and intellectual virtue intersects with all of the others. If any one trait is off-target, the others will be too. Character traits are like the threads of a spider web. Tugging on one affects all of the others.

Oh What a Tangled Web

It is easiest to demonstrate House's systemic character illness by focusing on his pathological obsession with the truth. So let's tug on this thread of House's web and see what happens. House's excessive desire for truth makes him unjust; he cares too much about finding the truth and not enough about other people's rights. In "DNR," House's patient is a famous horn player who has been diagnosed with ALS by another doctor. House chooses to violate his "Do Not Resuscitate" order (by intubating him and treating him for Wegener's disease) because he wants to figure out whether he was misdiagnosed with ALS. In "Human Error," House treats a patient who was rescued from the ocean while emigrating from Cuba. She dies, but he keeps her on bypass for hours, without telling her husband that she has died, because he wants to solve the case. Cuddy asks House: "Other than your curiosity, do you have any reason to keep her on bypass? Do you want a storybook ending? . . . I know you care." House replies: "I don't care. My motives are pure." That is, he cares only about the truth, not about the husband's right to know that his wife has died. Driven by his excessive desire for truth, House also routinely violates patients' rights to privacy by covertly sending his team into their homes to collect evidence. House's choices demonstrate that he does not care enough about other people's rights, their privacy, or their autonomy. Consequently, he is not just.

House's excessive desire for truth also makes him inappropriately cruel to his "friends" and patients. In "Whac-A-Mole," Tritter pressures Wilson (arguably, House's friend) to tell the truth about House's Vicodin addiction by revoking Wilson's license to prescribe medications. House agrees to send Cameron to write prescriptions for Wilson, but later refuses on the grounds that he needs Cameron to help solve his own case. House is also well-known for behaving cruelly toward patients and their families in order to extract information from them. House's choices demonstrate that he does not care enough about the welfare of other people. Consequently, he is not benevolent.

House's excessive desire for truth likewise makes him rash. House cares too much about finding truth and too little about risks. He is too quick to take chances and to "experiment" with patient care. For instance, in "Maternity," House decides to treat two sick babies with different medications in order to determine the source of their infection and prevent it from spreading. He knows that one of the babies will die. If House had fully informed each set of parents of all of the details of his approach and gained their consent, then his treatments may well have been courageous. But since he did not inform the parents, his treatments were rash, rather than courageous or admirable.

Granted, House often does what the intellectually virtuous person would do, and he does care about truth for its own sake rather than for the sake of money or fame. But since his motivation for truth is excessive, House falls short of full-blown intellectual virtue. Valuing the truth too much also affects the rest of what House values. And since, according to the Unity Thesis, all of the virtues (moral and intellectual) intersect, House is a man without virtue.

He's Sick, but Not That Sick

Is it possible that we have diagnosed House too quickly? What's the differential diagnosis? Could it be that House's character illness is localized and not systemic and that, therefore, though he lacks moral virtue, he still possesses intellectual virtue? If so, then the Unity Thesis would be false, and it would be possible to be simultaneously morally bad (or morally deficient) and intellectually good.

A strong case can be made that House has what's required for intellectual virtue, namely, enduring intellectual character traits. House cares about truth for its own sake, he reliably forms true beliefs, and he possesses open-mindedness, intellectual courage, and care in gathering evidence.

While there may be some question about whether House cares too much about the truth, there's no question that he cares about truth for its own sake. Unlike many of the other specialists on the show, House is unconcerned with money or status. But House doesn't just *care* about truth; he achieves it, which is to say that he consistently solves seemingly impossible cases that have stumped everyone else, and comes up with successful courses of treatment. He's able to do this by habitually behaving in ways that are open-minded, intellectually courageous, and careful in collecting evidence. Reliably forming true beliefs through these behaviors, out of concern for truth for its own sake, seems sufficient for intellectual virtue.

House's Open-Mindedness

In order to pursue the truth, House exercises specific intellectual virtues. To begin with, he is consistently open-minded. He is willing to consider multiple hypotheses and explanations for various medical problems even when they appear to others to be far-fetched. He thinks outside the box far more than the other doctors on the show, who tend to concentrate on obvious explanations, dismissing the more outrageous possibilities or those that would implicate patients and their families. For example, in the episode "Clueless," a young man is referred to House for an unusual cluster of symptoms. After the team rules out the most likely causes, House hypothesizes that the man is suffering from heavy metal toxicity. Since tests have ruled out exposure to any metals that could get into the air or water, House concludes that the man's wife must be poisoning him. The team is incredulous and resistant. House defends his ostensibly implausible explanation to Cameron: "It's the only explanation. We've eliminated every other possibility. It's not lupus. It's not allergies. It's not ALS, arthritis, or sarcoidosis. She's all that's left." Later, as House tries to convince Cuddy to authorize a search of the woman's body against Cameron's wishes, House again claims that the only explanation for the man's condition is that his wife is poisoning him. Cameron responds that "it's the only explanation your twisted mind can come up with." The explanation may be twisted, but it also turns out to be correct.

Although House frequently considers unconventional explanations, he doesn't listen to everyone or consider every alternative. Rather, he routinely discounts what patients voluntarily report about their lives and lifestyles, reasoning that what they say cannot be trusted, since "everybody lies." House's team and many of his patients are frustrated by his unwillingness to take patients' stories seriously. But the open-minded person doesn't listen to everyone. She listens only to those it's appropriate to listen to. House's suspicions about his patients' veracity almost always turn out to be correct. Think of all the patients on the show who lie about something relevant to their conditions: the father who has had sex with his daughter in "Skin Deep," the overworked supermom who lies about taking Ritalin and birth control pills in "Need to Know," and the young woman who lies about being allergic to a dog her girlfriend gave her in "Sleeping Dogs Lie." These are just some of the patients whose stories turn out to be untrustworthy. By being skeptical, House is able to diagnose and treat his patients more quickly and more effectively.

House's Intellectual Courage

House is intellectually courageous. He repeatedly stands up for his beliefs in the face of criticism and pressure from other doctors. Recall the episode "Safe" in which no one can figure out why Melinda, a teenage girl who has recently received a transplant, has gone into anaphylactic shock. After several treatments fail and Melinda continues to worsen, House concludes that she must be allergic to ticks and that there must be a tick somewhere on her body. No one wants to listen to House. They have already checked Melinda for insect bites. The tick theory is considered a waste of valuable time. Cuddy orders House to leave the room, but House is certain about his conclusion and won't back down. Ultimately, he traps Melinda in an elevator as they are wheeling her to the OR. As her heart rate continues to drop, he coerces Foreman into using his last shot of atropine to buy House a bit more time to find the tick. Just as Foreman restarts the elevator and Cuddy and Melinda's parents start to go crazy, House finds the tick that's responsible for Melinda's problems. It was inside her vagina (a place no one else looked).

While House often appears to delight in besting others in coming up with explanations for various conditions, he almost always gives up his views when there is good evidence against them or when someone has persuaded him that a particular view is incorrect. He runs his team meetings by brainstorming with his team about possible diagnoses and relevant explanations and then working to eliminate as many hypotheses as possible. For example, in the episode "Distractions," House hypothesizes that a teenage boy who has been badly burned in an ATV accident is suffering from depression. He continues to defend this hypothesis in the face of criticism until he finds a burn mark on the boy's wrist that suggests a different explanation. He immediately drops the depression hypothesis. Although House is egomaniacal, he cares more about truth than he does about being right.

Maggots, Break-ins, Whatever It Takes

In addition to being open-minded and intellectually courageous, House is careful in gathering evidence. Rarely, if ever, does he stop searching for evidence prematurely, and often when others have given up on solving some difficult case, House devises creative and unconventional methods to gather information, buy time for analyzing and evaluating information, and come up with accurate diagnoses and successful treatments.

For example, again in the episode "Distractions," the patient's burns are so bad that the normal tests that would be used to acquire diagnostic information cannot be done. So House has the team use a galvanometer, a device from the turn of the century that detects electrical currents. Later, when it's unclear whether the patient's infection is in his forebrain or his burned skin, House has his team put thousands of maggots on the patient's chest to eat the dead flesh and clean the wound. This gruesome technique keeps the team from having to wait for the burns to heal in order to find the source of the infection.

House regularly has the members of his team break into patients' homes to search for clues to their conditions. This method proves to be so effective that Foreman uses it in "Failure to Communicate" and in "Deception," when he is serving as the temporary supervisor of House's department. This is significant because Foreman is arguably the harshest critic of House's tendency to break the rules. Yet both of the times that Foreman orders the team members to break into patients' homes, the information obtained turns out to be important for solving the cases. House's methods might seem overzealous, but they frequently lead to truth by providing information critical for solving cases and treating patients.

Disunity of the Virtues?

Clearly House possesses at least some of the intellectual virtues, which means that the Unity of Virtues Thesis must be false. House is intellectually virtuous in spite of lacking moral virtue.

Perhaps in some cases or some domains, the lack of moral virtue creates problems for intellectual pursuits, but House's lack of moral virtue doesn't appear to interfere with his ability to acquire true beliefs. His lack of benevolence and honesty makes him a jerk, but it doesn't prevent him from being open-minded, intellectually courageous, or careful in gathering evidence.

His intellectual virtues don't make House a morally good person and don't lead him to treat people respectfully or with kindness and sensitivity, but the goal of intellectual virtue is not the appropriate treatment of others. It's truth. The intellectually virtuous person must care about truth for its own sake. House does.

Prognosis: Do We Really Want a Healthy House?

House is both a world-class jerk and a world-class diagnostician. He consistently employs creative and unconventional methods to acquire information and diagnoses that enable him to save patients with problems no one else can solve. The contrast between his failure at interpersonal interactions and his success at diagnostic medicine comes up over and over again in the show. Foreman describes him as a "manipulative bastard," but also as "the best doctor he's ever worked with."

What's more, if House possessed moral virtue—if he were a better person—he would not be a better doctor. He'd be a worse doctor. Thus if House were cured of his character illness, he would become less effective at curing his patients.

Wilson makes this point in the episodes "Euphoria, Parts 1 and 2," when House is trying to diagnose Foreman, who has developed a mysterious and deadly brain illness. Wilson questions House about his methods and says that House is being "cautious" and "common" because the patient is Foreman. As Foreman's condition worsens and time begins to run out, Foreman tells House to do a white-matter brain biopsy, which is an extremely dangerous procedure that could permanently damage Foreman's higher brain processes. House refuses to do the procedure, insisting that it's too dangerous and that they have more time. When Wilson finds out, he says that House is not proceeding as he normally would because he cares too much about Foreman. Trying to push House, Wilson says to him: "You don't see patients because then you'd give a crap and if you gave a crap, you wouldn't make the outrageous decisions you do." Wilson says that if it were any other patient, House would have damned the risks and done the procedure.

Experiencing sympathy toward his patients and investing in them as individuals would make it impossible for House to practice medicine the way he does. He would be more worried about the risks he regularly takes to acquire information about their conditions, and less willing to subject them to emotional and physical pain and suffering in order to get information. Empirical research shows that the people most likely to be sympathetic are susceptible to emotional overarousal when others are suffering, which makes them less able to help the people they sympathize with.[3]

House's dishonesty and his willingness to break the law are also essential to his regular method of diagnosis. House frequently breaks into his patients' homes to search for clues to their conditions. Breaking into patients' homes is an invasion of privacy, but it's one that very often produces information that turns out to be essential to solving a case. This happens in the very first episode of the show. House sends Foreman and Cameron to the home of a kindergarten teacher with several unexplained symptoms. Just when it seems that they have nothing to go on, House learns that the patient had ham in her refrigerator, which leads him to conclude that she has a tapeworm in her brain. He's right, as usual, but he's able to reach his conclusion only because of information he has acquired from breaking into her home. This method of gathering information is obviously inappropriate, not to mention illegal. Nevertheless, it's extremely effective.

These are just a few of the ways in which House's lack of moral virtue helps him to come up with accurate diagnoses that save his patients. Rare is the case where he doesn't employ deceptive and insensitive methods to save his patient against all odds. In other words, House's being a morally bad person is part of what makes him such an exceptional doctor.

What explains House's personality? Why is he so willing to do things that other people wouldn't? Why does he take so many risks? Because he is obsessed with figuring out his cases, finding answers to difficult questions, and coming up with diagnoses when other people cannot. This obsession leads him to break rules, treat people with cruelty and insensitivity, invade people's privacy, lie to people, and subject patients to risks that other doctors would judge too great. It makes him an outstanding diagnostician. But at what cost?

House has no life outside of his career. He has no partner, no real friends other than Wilson (whom he treats terribly), and no control over his serious drug addiction. As a result, he has very little to live for other than his success in solving cases and saving patients. These are worthy things, to be sure, but they are not sufficient for a full life. Okay, so House is obsessed. What should we conclude from this, and how does it relate to the issue of virtue? The kind of greatness that House exhibits as a diagnostician is possible only because his life is out of balance. He is able to be the very best doctor that Foreman has ever worked with, the doctor Cuddy describes as the best she has, and the doctor who fixes things when everyone else has failed because he is obsessed with finding the truth and with solving his cases. This obsession is all he has. It's his whole life.

House fascinates us in part because he is so good at his job and so bad at just about everything else and because these two facts seem related. Would we want House to be a better person? Not if we were suffering from some mysterious ailment. In that case, we would gladly endure his rudeness, his dishonesty, and his willingness to break the law.[4]

NOTES

1. House's diagnostic skills are not reliable in the sense that they produce more true beliefs about his patients' illnesses than false ones. Since House typically gets his patients' diagnoses wrong several times before he figures out the real problem, he ends up with more false beliefs than true ones. But he is reliable in the sense that he *eventually* attains true beliefs, in the form of correct diagnoses, about their illnesses—he solves every case.

2. Aristotle, *Nicomachean Ethics*, trans. David Ross (New York: Oxford Univ. Press, 1998), Book 2.6, 1006b36.

3. See Nancy Eisenberg, "Empathy and Sympathy," in *Handbook of Emotions*, ed. Michael Lewis and Jeanette M. Haviland-Jones (New York: Guilford Press, 2000); Nancy Eisenberg and Paul Miller, "Empathy, Sympathy, and Altruism: Empirical and Conceptual Links," in *Empathy and Its Development*, ed. Nancy Eisenberg and Janet Strayer (Cambridge: Cambridge Univ. Press, 1987); Martin Hoffman, *Empathy and Moral Development* (New York: Cambridge Univ. Press, 2000); and E. Ann Kaplan, "Vicarious Trauma," in *Empathy: Philosophical and Psychological Perspectives*, ed. Amy Coplan and Peter Goldie (Oxford: Oxford Univ. Press, forthcoming).

4. We are extremely grateful to our families and friends for helpful discussions and for commenting on earlier drafts: Rob Battaly, Trudy Battaly, Bettie Coplan, Shirley Coplan, Tobyn De Marco, Marco Iacoboni, Katie Kruse, Cori Miller, Ryan Nichols, Clifford Roth, and Margie Roth.

CONTRIBUTORS

Princeton-Plainsboro Teaching Hospital Staff

Jerold J. Abrams is associate professor of philosophy at Creighton University in Omaha, Nebraska. He writes regularly on the philosophy of film and popular culture, and his essays have appeared in various volumes: *Battlestar Galactica and Philosophy* (Blackwell, 2007); *The Philosophy of Film Noir*, *The Philosophy of Neo-Noir*; and *The Philosophy of Martin Scorsese* (University Press of Kentucky). Unlike House, Abrams walks perfectly, leaving him no good excuse for his rotten personality.

Jeremy Barris is professor of philosophy at Marshall University in Huntington, West Virginia. As a philosopher, he is mainly interested in the relations between reality, thinking, style of expression, humor, and justice. His publications include *Paradox and the Possibility of Knowledge: The Example of Psychoanalysis* and *The Crane's Walk: Plato, Pluralism, and the Inconstancy of Truth*. He likes to hit random strangers really hard with his walking stick, to see if that will help him solve the problem.

Heather Battaly is associate professor of philosophy at California State University, Fullerton. She was lucky to have a mathematician and a historian as her parents. This explains two of her greatest philosophical loves—logic and Aristotle—and her devotion to teaching. Her published work focuses on the theory of knowledge and intellectual virtue. She is the author of "Teaching Intellectual Virtues" in *Teaching Philosophy* (2006); and "Intellectual Virtue and Knowing One's Sexual Orientation" in *Sex and Ethics*, edited by R. Halwani (2007); and coeditor of *Perspectives on the Philosophy of William P. Alston* (2005). While she loves Dr. House, no amount of Vicodin could get her to take Cuddy's job.

Teresa Blankmeyer Burke teaches philosophy and bioethics at Gallaudet University in Washington, D.C., the world's only liberal arts college for deaf and hard-of-hearing people. She writes on bioethics and disability and is particularly interested in the potential consequences of genetic technologies on the signing Deaf community. Teresa secretly toys with the idea of using House's approach to differential diagnosis for evaluating her students, but she knows that Cuddy would never go for it.

Amy Coplan is assistant professor of philosophy at California State University, Fullerton. Her research interests include moral psychology, philosophy of film, and ancient Greek philosophy. She is currently coediting an interdisciplinary book on empathy (and yes, she knows what House would think of this) and editing a book on *Blade Runner*. Besides philosophy and movies, she enjoys cultivating her parasocial relationships with people like House and Wilson, telling people how incredible her two Labradors are (an objective fact, by the way), and diagnosing the personality disorders of her friends and family. Given House's misanthropic tendencies and caustic manner, she thinks he would fit right in at a meeting of the American Philosophical Association.

Jane Dryden is not a medical doctor with an electric guitar in her office, but she does have a doctorate in philosophy and a banjo. As she spends most of her time by herself in the library, she wishes she had a team of hot assistants to help her with her research, which focuses on German idealism and feminist philosophy. Jane thinks Hugh Laurie does a terrific job with his British accent on *Jeeves and Wooster*.

Kenneth Ehrenberg is assistant professor of philosophy and research associate professor of law at the State University of New York at Buffalo. He has published in legal theory, meta-ethics, and value theory, and is currently working issues involving authority and the methods we use to understand the law. He noted House's indebtedness to Sherlock Holmes the first time he saw the show and currently has only two degrees of separation from Hugh Laurie.

John R. Fitzpatrick teaches philosophy at the University of Tennessee at Chattanooga. He is the author of *John Stuart Mill's Political Philosophy: Balancing Freedom and the Collective Good* (Continuum Press, 2006), and the forthcoming *Starting with Mill* (Continuum Press, 2009). He has long been a fan of medical and mystery movies and is a National Master Chess player. Like House, John finds it easy to practice the virtue of eccentricity.

Like everyone who always wanted to become a physician, **Melanie Frappier** never applied to medical school, did an undergraduate degree in engineering physics, and then switched to philosophy. She happily taught in Mankato, at Minnesota State University, before going on to teach the history of science at the University of King's College in Halifax, Canada, where she still awaits her first appointment in a research hospital. Like House, she believes that the Socratic method is the best way to teach anything, but being the Canadian that she is (eh!), she doesn't dare make use of it in case she would offend someone. She lives in Nova Scotia with her husband and two sons.

David Goldblatt is professor emeritus of philosophy at Denison University in Granville, Ohio, and is the author of *Art and Ventriloquism* (Routledge) and is coeditor with Lee B. Brown of *Aesthetics: A Reader in Philosophy of the Arts* (Prentice Hall), now in its second edition. He is the author of a large number of philosophical articles, especially in the area of aesthetics; takes no prescription drugs; and believes that the less he knows about the internal working of his anatomy, the better.

Henry Jacoby teaches philosophy at East Carolina University in Greenville, North Carolina. He has published articles on philosophy of mind, language, and religion, and on the nature of moral perception. He also contributed to the volume on *South Park and Philosophy*. Like House, he has been alienating people since he was three.

Renee Kyle is an associate research fellow in the philosophy program at the University of Wollongong, Australia. Her research interests include feminist philosophy, moral psychology, trauma-related disorders, embodiment, and women's health. She is currently researching the ethical implications of nanotechnology, but she still spends every Tuesday waiting for Chase to ask her out.

Jennifer L. McMahon is associate professor of English and philosophy and chair of the English and Languages Department at East Central University in Ada, Oklahoma. Her areas of specialization include existentialism, philosophy and literature, aesthetics, and comparative philosophy. She has published articles in journals and anthologies. Her recent research has focused on popular culture and philosophy. Though she writes extensively on the works of existentialist Jean-Paul Sartre, Jennifer denies subscribing to Sartre's assertion "Hell is other people." However, she does agree with Gregory House that "everybody lies."

Sara Protasi likes philosophy so much that she is a graduate student in philosophy for the second time, at Yale University. She has published articles and book reviews on ethics in Italian and is working on a research project that develops her previous dissertation on true love. Sara was worried that Foreman was going to steal her article, but she worried even more when House talked him out of it.

Jeffrey C. Ruff is a professor of religious studies at Marshall University in Huntington, West Virginia. As a scholar, he is interested in meditation traditions (especially Zen and Yoga) and mystical and poetic visionary experiences (and the rhetoric one uses to talk about such things). Both as an artist and a scholar, he is generally interested in creativity, process, and methods—generally how human beings think about, talk about, and practice creative, imaginative, or intellectual work. In courses or writing about Zen, instead of lecturing about the history of *kōans* and *kenshō*, he is far more likely to talk about chocolate cake, the squirrels on campus, or looking at the moon. House would hate him.

Catherine Sartin is a student in the graduate program in philosophy at the University of Florida in Gainesville. When she decides to grow up and get a real job, she plans to work on the ethics committee at a hospital (and uses this to justify watching every episode of House again and again as research). In the meantime, she is focusing on aspiring to something that is less than pure evil.

Barbara Anne Stock is an associate professor of philosophy at Gallaudet University in Washington, D.C. Her research and teaching interests include moral philosophy, medical ethics, early modern philosophy, and philosophy through science fiction. Inexplicably, Gallaudet has allowed her to warp the minds of unsuspecting freshmen with an interdisciplinary course called "The Meaning of Life, According to *House M.D.*"

She anxiously awaits a return appearance of the true star of the series, Steve McQueen.

Peter Vernezze is an associate professor of philosophy at Weber State University in Ogden, Utah. He is the author of *Don't Worry, Be Stoic: Ancient Wisdom for Troubled Times*, and coeditor of *The Sopranos and Philosophy* and *Bob Dylan and Philosophy*. He would like to find some way to apply House's theory of medical care to the academic world so that he could keep his job without having to see students.

Sara Waller is associate professor of philosophy at Case Western Reserve University in Cleveland, Ohio. She recently completed an animal training course at Shedd Aquarium, where she learned about assumptions made about animal minds while working with sea otters, sea lions, Beluga whales, and Pacific white-sided dolphins. More about her work on the philosophical implications of dolphin minds, communication, and vocalization can be found at www.case.edu/artsci/phil/cetacean/cetacean2.htm. Her areas of research are philosophy of neurology, philosophy of cognitive ethology, and philosophy of mind, as well as *House, M.D.* and *Buffy the Vampire Slayer*. She is hoping to be next in the long line of Wilson's wives: great sex, lots of attention, and when he ignores her until she leaves, she knows he will still be her friend.

Mark R. Wicclair is professor of philosophy and adjunct professor of community medicine at West Virginia University in Morgantown. At the University of Pittsburgh, he is adjunct professor of medicine and a member of the Center for Bioethics and Health Law faculty. A self-proclaimed "House junkie," Mark uses clips from the series for his undergraduate and medical school classes and professional presentations. When he isn't watching *House, M.D.* while working out on his elliptical machine or teaching, he writes on a variety of topics in bioethics. His publications include a book, *Ethics and the Elderly* (Oxford University Press), as well as numerous book chapters and journal articles. He is writing a book on conscientious objection in health care that will be published by Cambridge University Press. As an ethics consultant for two hospitals, Mark's primary guideline for doctors is as follows: don't treat your patients like House treats his.

INDEX OF DIFFERENTIAL DIAGNOSES